1986

JEWISH WRITING AND IDENTITY IN THE TWENTIETH CENTURY

Jewish Writing and Identity in the Twentieth Century

Leon Israel Yudkin

ST. MARTIN'S PRESS   NEW YORK

© 1982 Leon Israel Yudkin
All rights reserved. For information write:
St. Martin's Press, Inc., 175 Fifth Avenue, New York, N.Y. 10010
First published in the United States of America in 1982

Library of Congress Cataloging in Publication Data

Yudkin, Leon I.
 Jewish writing and identity in the twentieth century.

 Bibliography: p. 159.
 Includes index.
 1. Jewish literature—20th century—History and criticism. 2. Jews—
Identity. I. Title'
PN842.Y8   1982   809'.8924   82-827
ISBN 0-312-44234-3   AACR2

Printed and bound in Great Britain

CONTENTS

Acknowledgements

Preface

1. A Jewish Literary Identity   11

2. The Immigrant Experience in America   27

3. A Brief Spring: In the German World Between the Wars   45

4. In the Eye of the Revolution: Russia   59

5. Hebrew Literature Between Exile and Home   78

6. Is There a French Jewish Literature?   96

7. From the Periphery to the Centre in America   112

8. On the Fringes of Europe: The Italian Scene   129

9. A New Beginning: Israeli Literature   142

Bibliography   159

Index   165

With ever new affection to Mickey

ACKNOWLEDGEMENTS

My grateful thanks are due to the University of Manchester for its financial assistance enabling me to use research facilities available in the United Kingdom and abroad; to the Institute of Jewish Affairs, London; The Postgraduate Hebrew Centre, Oxford; Le Centre de Documentation Juive, Paris; Il Centro di Documentazione Ebraica Contemporanea, Milan; The Hebrew University, Jerusalem; and the University of Tel-Aviv for their kind assistance in the use of their documentation facilities.

To all those, unrecorded here, whose comments and writings have helped me to illuminate dark areas and to fill in yawning gaps of ignorance.

PREFACE

It may be thought strange to devote a book to a subject whose meaningful existence is in question, or where the definition is so problematic. Is a 'Jewish writer' a separate genus, as distinct from a writer who happens to be Jewish, as another might be Protestant or a third ginger-haired? And if there is such a species, how is it to be defined? Is it as a writer who writes out of the consciousness of being Jewish, as suggested by Ludwig Lewisohn, or one who addresses a Jewish readership as argued by Zeev Jabotinsky? Does anyone born Jewish necessarily fall into the category?

My intention here is not to present a thesis in theory and then to examine it, nor to argue about definitions. All the suggested definitions are partly right and partially insufficient. I am rather assuming the subject — as evidenced by the numerous diverse cases expressed over a range of instances and literatures. Jewishness can be the subject of polemic, a formative influence, the object of quest, the means of expression, or a source of horror. The place of Judaism within Jewishness is also problematic.

An interesting phenomenon is the way that the subject manifests itself so variously in different places. My method of treatment in this book is to posit a spectrum, with, at one end, an identity of the literature with the medium of expression as in Palestine/Israel; at the other end, an almost totally assimilated literature as in Italy, where the subject is nevertheless interesting. In between, there is a flourishing and recognisable though changing literature in Yiddish and English in the USA, a negative response to Jewishness but a recognition of its importance in literature in the USSR, a disputed but substantial issue in France, and literature as a sensitive but disguised antenna in German-speaking countries between the wars. In each case, it is a central theme in major work.

The scheme of the book is to examine the literature area by area, whilst retaining chronological coherence where possible. The aim of the book is not only to establish the subject's undeniable existence through description and analysis, but also to examine its nature and quality. These differ from place to place — and between one individual and another.

1 A JEWISH LITERARY IDENTITY

The Jewish writer in the post-Enlightenment (late nineteenth century) was faced with a spectrum of role possibilities. In so far as he was Jewish he might self-identify with the Jewish group and aim at his Jewish audience. In so far as he operated within the framework of a particular host nation, he might try to integrate into that national entity. He might use Yiddish or Polish or Russian (about 90 per cent of Jewry was East European before 1880), depending on the circumstances of his upbringing and background. But there was also, increasingly, an element of choice; not, certainly, totally free and uncircumscribed but growing, with the increased mobility and accessibility to world events. This element of marginality, the possibility of personal identification, selection of audience and cultural loyalty, is not unknown to writers of other backgrounds, but it particularly confronted the Jewish writer. Could he simply write in the language of his country, aiming at that readership? This is a question that most nationals would not usually ask. There was normally a coincidence of language, culture, affiliation, nation and religion. Few languages were emotionally neutral. Polish, for example, was not only the language of a geographical region, but the medium of expression for a repressed and aspirant group after the repeated division and subjugation of Poland in the late eighteenth and early nineteenth centuries. Russian was the language of a great literature, but also of a Christian and anti-Semitic culture. German and French too had their own traditions, and were much associated with particular national ambitions.

For the Jew, there could be no simple selection then, even on this primary issue of language. Language could in itself constitute an ideology. To write in a non-Jewish language could imply not only association with and appeal to a certain readership, but also a shared community and fate. On the other hand, selection of a Jewish language was also fraught with difficulties. The predominant Jewish vernacular in Eastern Europe was Yiddish but this had a restricted literary tradition and its own drawbacks as far as the Jewish world, Jewish culture and the Jewish future were concerned. Hebrew was considered by many to be *the* Jewish language, in terms of its history, its Jewish quintessence and universality, and its potential (ideologically seen) if

11

revived. But there was a very small readership for Hebrew, and a Hebrew writer, like any other, needs his readers. We will try to examine the range of answers to the questions, implicit or explicit, offered by some Jewish writers of the period. Clearly, these answers will be governed, to some extent, by already determined factors, such as mother-tongue and background, but also by selection and (even of unstated) ideology too. Such answers indicated the way in which the Jewish writer saw himself and his function, his society (or societies), his and the group's future, and his and the group's aspirations.

The post-Enlightenment era had torpedoed the Jew into a world of options, or, at least, temptations. His place was no longer a permanent datum within a rigidly patterned religious culture. Henceforth, he was to be a Jew (to whatever extent) and something else too, whether national or international, unitarily cultural or cross cultural. It has been suggested that the Jewish background could have considerable implications in this post-religious realm. For example, with regard to art for art's sake, one critic has written:

> The Jews here had no tradition of aesthetics as an *autonomous realm*, no historically rooted notion of the poet as hero and guide. Some Jewish writers seem vaguely uncomfortable with the very idea of artistic originality even as they aspire to it, as though it were something they had filched from European Romanticism without ever being quite sure of the genuineness of the article. (Alter)

There is certainly great literature in the Bible, but the spring of the work is passionately religious rather than aesthetic. The Rabbinic tradition had as its object clarification of a Jewish role in observance of commandments, in explication of revealed texts and God's functioning, not the recounting of fables for their own sake. And so too with the main direction of medieval literature, whether 'religious' or 'secular'. Even those who moved away from the tradition were conditioned by it within the terms of the rhetoric devised and adopted. Could it be that the meta-aesthetic character of Jewish conditioning continued to control the concerns of the Jewish writer and his unconscious aspirations in the world of modern, positivist secularism?

There can be no single answer to this question. There is not only a multiplicity of individuals involved, but an unevenness of development, assumptions about the readership, culture and truth as various as the languages. The degree of integration of the Jew was so different in *fin-de-siècle* Paris and Vienna from that of, for example, the Ukraine and Lithuania. Conditions were rapidly changing too, both without, with new nationalisms, a struggling proletariat, population growth, and within, in terms of local Jewish exposure to the outside world, and its own aspirations, whether towards religious expression (Hasidism, Talmudism, Reform, etc.), towards integration (Liberalism, Socialism, Capitalism) or towards Jewish nationalism (Bundism, Zionism). We will examine a few particular cases.

Shalom Yaakov Abromowitz, popularly known as Mendeli Mocher Sefarim (1836-1917) has the unique distinction of being known as the founder of two modern literatures — Yiddish and Hebrew. A lexicon of Yiddish literature says of him that 'not only is he a great original Yiddish writer but is altogether the first great artist in Yiddish . . . he raised Yiddish literature from its low rank' (Rejzen). And the Hebrew poet H.N. Bialik, in two essays dealing with Mendeli's status as a Hebrew author, written after the appearance of the three volume edition of Mendeli's work in 1912, writes that, 'when you read Mendeli's writing, you get the constant feeling that you are confronted not merely with the work of an artist but with a "first", with all the significance of that word for us Jews' ('Mendeli ushloshet hakrakhim'). 'First' indicates the authority that inheres in the earlier interpretation, the classical source, which in traditional Jewish hierarchical status is not only primary in chronology but in weight too. Bialik also claims for Mendeli that he, single-handed, created a new standard language which became the basic tool of Hebrew literature henceforth ('yotzer hanusah'). Hitherto, the language of modern Hebrew literature had been a pastiche of quotations and archaic forms. Mendeli, even without the use of the live vernacular, had incorporated all layers of the language, plus Aramaic and the flavour of spoken Yiddish, into a new integrated whole.

Mendeli's status as the founder of both literatures has not been challenged. Born in the province of Minsk, he appropriated and transformed the two potential Jewish linguistic traditions in order to reach his audience. He clearly wrote about and for a Jewish readership, whether in fun or with mordant criticism. One of the sources for our knowledge of his background is his short autobiographical statement of 1889 ('reshumoth letholdothay') where he discusses the springs of his inspiration, his background and some of his literary aims. Until the age of 13, 'there was nothing in my world except Jewish law, and I knew nothing apart from the Talmud'. But in addition, he had been much moved by his natural home environment; nature always provided relief from and contrast to the grinding poverty and meanness of the small town. It was this contrast that galvanised him into writing in the first place, and then suggested the content and tone. Mendeli was didactic in the Enlightenment spirit, seeking to reprove and improve and his first impulse was to use the 'holy tongue' for the telling of the tales that fascinated him. That, after all, was 'Israel's source'. But after some experience in this vein, he came to the regrettable if obvious conclusion that 'most of them do not know this language, but speak Jewish-German. What is the purpose of a writer labouring so if he achieve nothing?' He must have an audience. So to reach his particular audience, he had to turn to Yiddish. Although, here too lay a difficulty.

> Yiddish in my time was an empty vessel containing nothing positive, just a lot of drivel, rubbish and worthlessness created by anonymous halfwits without command of language, read by women and the impoverished without understanding, and the rest, even if they knew no other language, would be ashamed to let on that they were reading such stuff.

So Hebrew was unknown and Yiddish was degraded. To reach his readership, Mendeli from about 1862 onwards made a conscious move to Yiddish, without abandoning his first loyalty (the first edition of the Hebrew novel *haavoth vehabanim* appeared in 1866). Later, from just before his autobiographical statement, from 1886 onwards, he returned to Hebrew writing.

But this third stage, the second Hebrew phase, is the one so praised by Bialik. His early Hebrew writing is in the mould of the early 'modern', resetting already formed phrases in the context of contemporary narrative, and adopting a quasi-Biblical flavour, without the Biblical impetus. The success of the new Mendeli lay in his incorporation of his Yiddish achievements in Hebrew guise, to create a quite different, more flexible and live language. His second Hebrew phase consisted mainly of recasting his Yiddish works. In Yiddish, the author had adopted the narrative persona of the 'bookseller' by which he was to be known. The bookseller (mocher sefarim) is often the narrator and a major character in his tales. As an itinerant, he can observe the scene in all its forms, throughout the Pale of Settlement. This process of observation became the overt direction of the writing, the bearer not so much of the specificity of place, character and incident, as of the general in those features noted. He makes the sweeping comment in *sefer haqabtzanim* (*book of beggars*, 1909): 'all Israel is a beggar', effecting a sweeping characterisation of contemporary Jewry. His first Hebrew story in the new mode, 'beseter raam' (1886), introduces the Hebrew reader to 'Kisalon' (literally 'fooltown'), not carrying individual features but looking like every Jewish town. 'This Kisalon, with which I am opening my story, is particularly important in that wherever Jews live, is thus called . . . Kisalon is a completely Jewish town in all ways. There is no respect for architecture, its houses do not stand and are unpainted. Beauty and grace are considered unworthy, and thus not worth a brass farthing.' The adoption of the bookseller's guise enables the author to roam freely and to generalise. And this generalisation is made on the basis of comparison, and is critical. He is both in and yet not completely of the passing scene. He belongs culturally, and yet can observe (as he thinks) with detachment and so utterly pulverise his target, as he does in his early works (he was later to soften his tone considerably).

Yiddish had the virtue of being understood by the Jewish masses. Hebrew was the adored (holy) language of all sections of the Jewish people and of all historical phases. The author, often moving from one to the other, split in loyalty and purpose, attempted to merge the two, and so began to create a new readership.

If Mendeli created a tool for the rendering of the Jewish collective in fiction, his younger contemporary, Micha Josef Berdyczewski (1865-1921), was more concerned with the Jewish individual. Particularly with that rebellious individual, moving beyond the confines of the particular Jewish world in search of a larger world and personal spiritual and intellectual fulfilment. Born in Medzibezh, Podolia, where the Jewish population in 1897 was recorded at 6,040, i.e. 73.9 per cent of the total (it was then Russian Ukraine), he spent his early youth in Dubow, Kiev, but then moved out of the Pale altogether, to Germany; Breslau in 1890 and Berlin in 1892. He was to spend the rest of his life almost entirely in Germany and Switzerland, writing in Yiddish and German, although mainly in Hebrew, stories, essays and controversial reconstructions of Jewish history, proposing an antithesis to mainstream Judaism in an undercover tradition that had been, in his view, repressed by Rabbinism.

This brief biographical sketch contains both the typical and the unique. Typical is the author's tone, rebellious against the limitations of his background and environment, yet firmly attached to the umbilical cord of Jewish history, fate and language. Unusual though is his ploughing of the Hebrew field (most of his work is in Hebrew, including about 150 stories) far from the traditional centres of Jewish culture and readership. This situation is indeed a prominent subject of his, as in, for example, the cycle of stories 'mihutz latehum' ('beyond the pale'). Here the name suggests the theme, and the central character is very like the author — a poverty-stricken, intellectually aspirant, spiritually dissatisfied and restless young Jew, moving from Eastern Europe to the West in search of education, new truths and personal contacts. He wants to penetrate this fascinating foreign world of universities and beautiful Gentile girls without complexes, but he is all the time aware of the great divide, as when he describes the great city in his story 'mahanayim' ('two camps') on 'their Sabbath'. The Jewish student is cast as 'uprooted', i.e. out of his natural environment and transplanted, albeit of his own volition, to foreign soil. Not with total success. He is like an anchorite 'in this bustling city with its bustling life', entirely given over to his own thoughts and imaginings. But in spite of this detachment and submission to his ambitions, he still yearns to be part of the life that he witnesses, to be freed from this marginality. At the ice rink: 'Amongst all the skaters, male and female, there is no-one who knows him. To all of them he is foreign, strange.' His situation had been different: 'He had been totally of his own heritage and observing it. Now·he had moved out of its sphere and striven to obliterate everything there acquired, going from darkness to light, from slavery to freedom.' From the world of the Jew, he had shifted to the world of man, in search of the universal. but can he find it? Apparently 'nothing had remained with him of his people, yet he was a son to his people. His brain had been emptied of his heritage, but his heart was still wedged in the grave of his ancestors.' The tragedy lies not so much in the preclusive attraction of the two worlds, as in the assumption that he will never wholly belong to either. He yearns for the life that he observes, and for the simple Hedwig who loves him. But, in great self-disgust, he finds that he has to leave her in search of greener pastures in Berlin. He has lost both the girl and himself.

The label of 'young' seemed to adhere permanently to Berdyczewski. He had become associated with a vanguard attacking the conservatism of Ahad-Haam (1856-1927) and seeking a broader base for a renascent Hebrew culture: 'The place is constricted for us. The time has come to find our way and go forth' (*hashiloah,* 1, 1896). He wanted to allow expression to 'all the new forces, wills and values stirring within us'. Ahad-Haam was cautious about the Hebrew language and its use, seeking to conserve and develop it through gradualism.

Berdyczewski, on the other hand, was revolutionary, looking for change and overflow of the old. He was sure that there was a potentially different readership available now. But his stories, usually constructed as chronicles, stress the weight and force of the past. Even the principal characters are not free-floating individuals hovering in their own space, but conditioned by genealogy and fate. The story 'kalonymos ve noomi' ('Kalonymos and Naomi') for example, treats not only of the two named characters, but of their antecedents and destiny. They are close and their union should make an ideal match, but as in S. Ansky's *The Dybbuk* (1919), the union is averted. When it does come, it is too late. (In *The Dybbuk*, the wrong match transpires, and the bride is possessed by the dybbuk of the departed lover.) Disaster has ensued, and the late match cannot fully repair the damage. Many of Berdyczewski's stories revolve around disaster irreparable. The theme of his very first story written in 1888, significantly entitled 'hetzitz venifga' ('he peeped and was stung') – a reference to the well-known Rabbinic story in B. Tal. Hagigah 14[B], where four entered the orchard, i.e. the firmament as traditionally understood, or the region of dangerous speculation, and one of them, Ben-Zoma 'peeped and was stung' – as its title suggests, deals with apostasy. Many of the author's heroes are young, disaffected Jews of traditional backgrounds, who become fascinated by unauthorised speculation, and so depart the tradition, also courting disaster. The story has the classical dimension of a specific event, embodying the direction of a determining Fate. The individual is an item in a larger context, and must play out his limited role within it. And the subject here is the characteristic Jew of the *fin-de-siècle*, uprooted from one culture, not at home in the new environment, and without a comfortable region of his own.

Mendeli and Berdyczewski were born into and wrote within a totally Jewish context. Even when they emerged from their little towns, their background defined their range and preoccupations. But there were other Jewish writers within the Russian Empire who were, to a degree, culturally assimilated and whose position was thus more ambiguous *a priori*. Vladimir Jabotinsky (1880-1940) was born in Odessa, initially wrote in the Russian language, and was accepted by the literary world as a Russian author of talent. Yet, he made a conscious decision to turn his back on the Russian language, because Russian literature implied a Russian context, specifically Orthodox Christian and anti-Semitic. When he opted for a local Jewish readership, his defection was considered a great loss to Russian literature by such as Maxim Gorky (Laqueur). In two essays originally written in Russian in 1908 and 1909 he puts the position of the Jew within Russian literature, but also, incidentally defines what a Jewish writer is.

In the earlier piece of occasional writing, 'On Jews and Russian Literature', he reacts to a current debate about the role of the Jew in Russian literature, and he states his frank and brutal conviction that the Jew has made no significant contribution. And he has made no such contribution because he simply does not belong there. Jabotinsky distinguishes between loyalty and love, and says that although one can and should be loyal to any place of residence, one can only love what is truly one's own. So a country can make a claim on your trust but not on your heart. The same applies, by extension, to culture generally and to literature. You operate freely and creatively in it, if it is your own. What is one's own, national literature? For Jabotinsky, it is not the linguistic medium that defines the national character of the literary work, nor for that matter the writer's origin, nor his subject. 'The decisive factor is the author's state of mind, whom is he aiming at when composing his work . . . not the language, but the intention is the main point.' In other words, a Jewish writer is one who writes in a Jewish spirit for a Jewish readership. Those others, at whom Jabotinsky now aims his darts, have gone over to the 'rich neighbour', i.e. to Russian literature. But such as Peretz and Bialik are 'ours', according to this view. However poor the prospect, the Jewish world makes a claim on those who would be loyal to their root! 'Someone has to stay.' He is willing to use any language that the Jew understands, whether it be Russian, Yiddish or, as he might hope, with the fulfilment of national aspirations, Hebrew. But he is a Jewish writer, because he is of the Jewish world and wants to stay there. Let those others who are willing to defect, delude themselves that the Russian world is theirs.

In the later essay 'The Russian Cares', he addresses himself specifically to the Jewish image in Russian literature. Jews now (i.e. in 1909) declare themselves surprised at Russian chauvinism. They had thought that the Russian or, at any rate, the Russian intellectual, was totally different from other nationals, and could not be anti-Semitic. As though the Russian intellectual, unlike his counterpart elsewhere, was, of necessity, a humane internationalist. As for inconvenient phenomena such as pogroms, these were attributed to the peasants below and reactionary bigots in power above. But, argues Jabotinsky, what goes on in a country is characteristic of the Nation in general, and Russian literature, especially as it is so much of the people, echoes typically Russian aspirations and tendencies. Although the Russians may be permeated with the notion of freedom in principle, they have held enslaved peoples in traditionally low regard. The specific case under discussion here is the great writer Nikolai Gogol (1809-52), the centenary of whose birth was just being celebrated. By Jews too, although that writer had incited pogroms against them. But he is not an isolated phenomenon. Pushkin, Turgenev, Dostoevsky, Chekhov — all have absurdly negative Jewish portraits, and the Jew hardly anywhere emerges positively. Both in fiction and non-fiction. There is no Russian equivalent, says Jabotinsky, of a Nathan the Wise or Shylock, of empathy with this lowly figure.

So, both as an image in Russian literature and himself on the Russian literary scene, the Jew has had either a negative or negligible role. Which leads Jabotinsky to turn inwards, and then in the direction of a resurgent Jewish nationalism. If the Jew is rejected by his host society, he must, in order to salvage self-respect, create a society of his own. And not merely a superstructure of incidental social, cultural or religious characteristics, but with its own infrastructure, soil and political independence. Jabotinsky is, of course, primarily remembered today as the breakaway leader of Zionist Revisionism, a nationalist maximalist who saw the constitution of Palestine as an independent Jewish state as the only possible salvation for the Jews in the threatening climate of the time. His only novel, *Samson* (1927), obliquely expresses that sort of aspiration. Samson, as we know from the Biblical story, was a powerful leader, strong and fascinating, although he did not totally succeed in uniting the people in victory against the Philistines. But in the novel, Samson offers his view of Philistine success: 'Where does their strength lie? In orderliness. Everything is measured and calculated beforehand. Every man knows his place. That is good.' The Philistines are few, but united and organised. Organisation and orderliness are vital for success. Samson says later, in Philistia, when he witnesses the power of the priest: 'He could not have given words to his thoughts, but he had a feeling that here, in this spectacle of thousands obeying a single will, he had caught a glimpse of the great secret of politically minded peoples.' He also appreciates the significance of resources, particularly of metal. This has Biblical support in the statement (Sam.1, 13:19) that 'no blacksmith was to be found in the whole of Israel, for the Philistines were determined to prevent the Hebrews from making swords and spears' (NEB). And Samson's last message to his people, in the novel, is 'Get iron and a king . . . And learn to laugh'. Jabotinsky has moved on from an estimate of the place and function of the Jewish writer at the beginning of the century to a political platform staking a claim to Jewish sovereignty in the Middle East.

In Western Europe too, there was a sense of Jewish identity or dissatisfaction with the possibilities of Jewish expression. Of course, the circumstances were different. There was not a defined Jewish society in any large sense after the disappearance of the legally imposed ghetto, the process of the Enlightenment and the French Revolution. Many Jews had moved from East to West, when that became possible, in search of advancement and education, and had naturally absorbed the characteristics of their host societies, including their customs and languages. The Jewish author writing in a European language therefore could not have a specifically Jewish audience in Jabotinsky's sense (with the limited exception of the local Jewish press), or in the way that he could if he wrote in Yiddish or Hebrew. Nevertheless, he often had a perceptible sense of a different loyalty or sense of identification. Sometimes, he had this ascribed to him, willy nilly. Max Nordau (1849-1923) is an interesting case in point. Later known as one of the founding fathers and spokesman of the Zionist Movement, he had already made a great name for himself as a physician and critic of culture (grand diagnostician). His books of the 1880s and 1890s had enormous currency, even when their circulation was restricted as a possible source of danger to the State. He applies an analytic apparatus to contemporary civilisation, and pronounces, perhaps absurdly lumping all cultural and literary phenomena together, that it is sick. Symptomatic are Baudelaire, Ibsen and Wagner. Religion is a fraud, charlatanism is rife, monarchy is a sham. All these deprivations of freedom are cited in *Die conventionellen Luegen der Kulturmenscheit* (1883, *The Conventional Lies of our Civilisation*, 1885) as a threat to true humanity. Although these could be cured, he concludes on an upnote: 'I see the civilisation of today, whose characteristics are pessimism, lying and selfish egotism, followed by a civilisation of truth, love of one's neighbour and cheerfulness. Humanity, which is today an abstract idea, will then be a fact. Happy the later-born generations, whose lot it will be to live in the pure atmosphere of the future, flooded with its brighter sunshine, in this perpetual fellowship; true, enlightened, good and free!'

There is no doubt that here, and more particularly in *Entartung* (1893, *Degeneration*, 1895), Nordau is guilty of distortion, oversimplification, over-optimism (when convenient) and even simple ignorance. G. B. Shaw, in his review of *Degeneration* entitled 'The Sanity of Art' (*Liberty*, 27 July 1895) finds that Nordau simply does not understand how poetry and art operate. He did not understand what Ibsen was doing, nor his moral principles and criticism, nor what

Wagner's music had achieved. But it is not the point at issue whether Nordau was right or wrong. We should ask ourselves rather where he stood in relation to contemporary society and culture. And both as critic and Zionist, he took a view apart from it. He was indeed a marginal case, and this was not lost on contemporary critics of his work. Bleibtrau, for example, asks whether Nordau was a Frenchman, a German or Hungarian. He is indeed 'a native Hungarian, has seldom visited Germany and has for a long time resided in Paris' (Ben-Horin). This is precisely the point. He came from Hungary, went to Austria, and lived in France. He wrote in German. And so he belonged nowhere unreservedly.

In brief, you might characterise him as a Jew, a category that breaches cultural and political walls. But it is a recognition that was to become increasingly central to this sort of marginal writer, physician and learned critic. He was of particular importance to Herzl in the Zionist Movement, from the first Zionist Congress in 1897, both as analyst of the contemporary Jewish situation and formulator of the draft programme. His, and for that matter, Herzl's, analysis of contemporary Jewry, is interesting, as proceeding from this West, where progress and emancipation had been enshrined for a full century. There was, as we have noted, no community in the Eastern sense, and, as yet, no pogroms. But strangely, in view of progressive hopes, anti-Semitism was on the increase, and the full force of the disappointed expectation was more perceptible in the West. Nordau, in his famous speech to the first Congress, said: 'The men of 1792 emancipated us only for the sake of principle', i.e. it was not a genuinely felt and deep emancipation, but only proceeding from the logic of the critical principle of equality for all men. The Jew now falls between two stools: 'He has lost the home of the ghetto: but the land of his birth is denied to him.' The medieval Jew might have been deprived, but at least he had a defined place, both for himself and in the regard of others. Now the picture is uniformly depressing, both materially and spiritually. There is material suffering in Eastern Europe, North Africa and Western Asia. And in Western Europe 'the misery is moral'. There is emancipation in law, but not in sentiment. Zionism is seen as the appropriate response for our own times, with the rise of nationalism generally, the raising of political consciousness, the failure of the Emancipation and the impossibility and undesirability of putting the clock back.

Let us see the Jewish writer from another perspective, although in similar context. The Viennese dramatist and writer of novellas, Arthur

Schnitzler (1862-1931) could not apparently suffer from cultural schizophrenia. He was born, grew up and functioned in Vienna, wrote German, and was one of the most successful writers of his time and environment, embodying that era and place for so many.

Schnitzler was fairly typical of the Viennese Jews in his background and origins. Although he was Viennese born, his father, originally named Zimmerman, a highly successful doctor, hailed from Hungary. The mass of Jews got to Vienna as the result of two things (although there had been the framework of a community since the twelfth century). One was the successive division of Poland in the late nineteenth century and, thus, the incorporation of Galicia within the Habsburg Empire. The other was the revolution of 1848 which permitted the free movement of Jews, and so led to migrations in the direction of Vienna on the part of the ambitious. Vienna was the political, commercial and cultural centre of the great Empire and flourished mightily under Franz-Josef. The Jewish community became typical of many in the Western world, embracing a wide variety of practice and sense of identification, increasing in numbers but considerably assimilating at the edges. The decades of the 1860s and 1870s were known for their liberalism, and Schnitzler dwells on this atmosphere in his memoirs. But he notes too the prevalent and indeed growing anti-Semitism of the later period, particularly at the end of the century: 'But when these pages may be read, it will perhaps no longer be possible to gain a correct impression (at least I hope so) of the importance, spiritually almost more than politically and socially, that was assigned to the so-called Jewish question when these lines were written. It was not possible, especially not for a Jew in public life, to ignore the fact that he was a Jew; nobody else was doing so, not the Gentiles and even less the Jews.'

So although Schnitzler grew up in a home almost totally devoid of Jewish practice, he was very aware of his Jewishness, associated by anti-Jewish feeling. His barmitzvah was celebrated without ritual, but still noted, even if just as a thirteenth birthday of somewhat greater significance than other birthdays. He did attend Jewish instruction, although during adolescence he regarded himself as an atheist. By the time he registered as a medical student, he noted a worrying xenophobia. The Vienna City Council turned anti-Semitic, with Lueger, the future mayor, adopting this plank as a piece of political opportunism rather than out of conviction. Jews had to take up duelling. Would they fight? 'The question was very topical at the time for us young men, especially for the Jews among us, since anti-semitism was spreading rapidly in student circles. The German-national associations, or Burschenschaften, had already started to expel all Jews and Jewish descendants.' So he observed the beginnings of German nationalism in Austria, which had the unexpected effect of creating an articulate and organised Jewish nationalism. 'One of the Jewish students who belonged to a German-national fraternity before the changes just mentioned, was Theodor Herzl. That they eventually expelled him, or, as the students called it, "bounced" him, was undoubtedly the first motivation that transformed this German-national student into the perhaps more enthusiastic than convinced Zionist, as which he lives in posterity.' He says little more of Herzl, except of a chance meeting later in England, and nothing more of the Jewish national movement. His associations, as he notes, were mainly with the 'solid Jewish bourgeois circles'.

These circles are noted for a behavioural quirk that was to figure much more prominently in Schnitzler's opus. It was the fashion there, claims our author, for love not to be consummated. The natural class associate of the aspirant Jewish doctor and littérateur was the counterpart, middle-class Jewish lady. But for her part, she would tend to withhold sexual gratification from the young men. So he had to find a lady of a special sort. She acquired her special identity from Schnitzler who labelled her the 'süsse Mädl' ('sweet maiden'). Before the young man felt ready and fit for marriage, he would adopt, at any rate in Schnitzler's writing, this 'sweet maiden' as a sexual companion. The mores of this class of society constitute a prominent subject. Schnitzler says that he coined the term 'süsse Mädl' in 1887, enjoyed life, and avoided the 'great issues' of God, war and nationalism. It is the 'small issues' that he writes about – passion, jealousy and hypocrisy. He took up an interest in hypnotism and in his compatriot co-religionist's work on psychoanalysis. He has sometimes immortalised those practices in classical form, as in the play *Reigen* (1900, *Merry-go-round*, 1952). The 'süsse Mädl' makes her appearance again, but as one of many enjoying the 'round' of sexual use, manoeuvre, exploitation, satisfaction and escape. The pride of conquest and achievement are placed above genuine feeling and attachment. All participants are playing a game, and in each of the ten dialogues or encounters, there is a winner and a loser, though both either lie or will lie at the next encounter. The one exception is the prostitute, who, with her particular social status, has no need to lie, and would derive no benefit from it. Lying, even to oneself, and the unconscious truth behind the action within the personal relationship, is at the heart of the Schnitzler tale.

He wrote for and beyond Viennese society, and avoided other issues, preferring to concentrate on his strong points or natural preoccupations. He modestly disclaims greatness in his self-estimate.

Schnitzler was writing in German and reaching Europe, Jew and non-Jew. Other Jewish writers struggled with the issue of stagnant or resurgent Jewish society, self-identification, the possibility of existential or social Jewish life, the form and language in which that could be cast, and the appropriate society to create in or country to live in. Yosef Haim Brenner (1881-1921) offered a despairing embrace to a Hebrew redivivus and to the possibility of a new Jewish Palestine. Originally from the Ukraine, he was in the Russian army from 1901 to 1904, later spent some years in London where he edited a Hebrew journal, then returned to Lvov on his way to Palestine, where he spent the years from 1909 until his demise in the Jaffa riots.

From his first publication in 1900, he wrote exclusively in Hebrew, developing an idiosyncratic, confessional, cultivatedly unpolished style. Following his hero Berdyczewski, he also set the uprooted, searching, dissatisfied individual at the centre of his stories. But he was above all interested in the individual psychopathology of the sick soul. Not in his antecedents, nor in rounded plot, nor in the overall context, but in the afflicted character's stream of consciousness, his struggles, his aspirations and despair. All in the contemporary Jewish situation which he would have liked to transform totally, as well as to jettison the tradition and imprint of the past. He sought a renaissance, but not a grand renaissance, just a mini-renaissance which would enable the Jew to live on his land and from his labour. The tragedy of his characters (and of himself for that matter) was that in this they were doomed to failure. They cannot even achieve the minimal, modest success of the average peasant, but are plagued by sickness, doubt, erotic failure, breakdown, personal tragedy and lack of successful human contact.

The Palestinian experience naturally interested him at all times, particularly so from the moment of his personal emigration. And in his writing too. So it is perhaps paradoxical that in a 'letter' (essay) of 1911, he attacks the 'Palestinian genre'. When asked whether a new story is set in Palestine 'a mocking feeling stirs within me, as though writing is, as it were, an external matter and not something inward, a revelation of inner life in all its essence within a particular context'. But the new Palestinian society would be difficult to record anyway in literature proper, because it is new, because it has not yet jelled: 'Insofar as it is the continuation of the diaspora, it is not interesting. And insofar as it is new, it lacks stability and typicality.' People, in fact, are asking for a revival in all respects. But this is not literature. As for himself: 'I only write letters where I relate to whomever is interested what sort of impressions I receive and how my days are spent in the Land.'

This is a literary pose. In the very year that he wrote the essay on the 'genre', he began writing in the genre itself. His story 'atzabim' ('Nerves') was also published in 1911, and is his first with a Palestinian setting. There is a story within a story, where an incident is related to the narrator concerning his arrival in Palestine. On the one hand, he plays down his excitement at the Land, in deprecation of the experience and in contrast to the more rooted life lived by genuine Europeans. He disparages the way he would write if he were 'one of those' who speak in typical vein of 'our colonies', 'treetops' and 'glimmering lights'. But in spite of his dismissal of beauty, he finds that he does genuinely believe in beauty. So he protects himself by irony. Brenner uses a similar technique in his Palestinian novel of the same year *Mikan umikan (From Here and There)*. The narrator has found diaries in a traveller's bag. He is seemingly reluctant to publish the material, because it is not romantic, not optimistic, not grand, not poetic, not polished. There are no gay portraits of joyful nationalists, exuberant youth babbling in the old/new Hebrew. On the contrary, it contains just the opposite — disorganised material in a low key proceeding from a disenchanted pen. So the novel is of this character — partial, disjointed and negative, to the extent that all romantic theses are challenged and rejected before the limited positive element can be carved out. Brenner's technique, through his narrators and characters, is to face the truth as brutally and totally as the human personality can allow, so that when a chink of light does peep through, it can be perceived as a genuine 'in spite of all'.

It is lives that form the content of Brenner's writing, the lives of his characters and of himself, who is a figure in his own fiction. On of his early works *Bahoref* (1902, *In the Winter*) is cast in the form of an autobiography, but so that the subject shall not seem inflated, it is an anti-autobiography of a non-hero. He opens with the act of writing: 'I made a notebook of clean paper to write some sketches and notes of my life. "My life" in inverted commas. I have no future or present, only the past ... my past is not that of a hero, because I am not a hero. Just a children's teacher in the village. Nevertheless, in spite of not being a hero, I want to write down this past of mine, the past of my non-heroism.' The author has summarised his own subject: non-heroism in the contemporary Jewish situation, with all the despair and aspiration attendant. He has selected an apparently negative subject for negative treatment, and addressed — what readership? Not even that tiny band of Hebrew readers fed on the classics and the Hebrew revival. He challenges every assumption, religious, historical, cultural and aesthetic. His readership is small, new, different, ready to accept his challenge. But the only one possible for him.

We have darted here round parts of the world at a particular period, looking at different writers of different backgrounds, writing in different languages out of different assumptions. There has been no intention to suggest a unified theme or approach. These are Jewish writers carving out literature from an experience, sometimes changing course, country, language, opinion and objective. They reflect the pattern of Jewish life made articulate.

THE IMMIGRANT EXPERIENCE IN AMERICA

Demographically, nothing has been more remarkable in Jewish history than the immigration to America. Within a hundred years (1825-1925), the American Jewish community was transformed from one of insignificant measure to the largest and most affluent in the world. Whereas within that span the American population in general increased tenfold, the Jewish population increased more than three hundredfold to four-and-a-half million (Gartner). The Jewish body, particularly that of New York, was remarkable for its size, for its freedom, for its relative wealth and for its growing power. The scale and suddenness of recent events brought two worlds into contrast and focused attention both on the differences between these two worlds and on the nature of Jewish identity. Jewish writers of the time could write about a Jewish situation or about an individual without extra-American historical ties. But the environment, spiritual as well as social, often held implications beyond what was publicly affirmed on the surface. Official policy, national ideology and outlook did not necessarily express deeper layers of ethnic instinct. There was a contrast observed between what the individual proclaimed as doctrine and between what he genuinely felt. Much of this Jewish writing articulates such perceptions and ambiguous situations. Jewish immigrants wanted to be in America (they chose to come). America wanted them, for their expansionist potential. But what was the meaning of American Jewishness or Jewish Americanism? Had the parties to the implied contract understood its terms, and how were they going to interpret them? The novels discussed here are not only fictions but also the vehicles for the deepest concerns of the writers.

The period we are dealing with coincides, not unexpectedly, with the emergence of America as a great world power. Facets of the new culture epitomise its generative force. New York, more than any other city in the world, served as a model for development or, negatively, as a a warning of the future. Modernisation meant Americanisation. Artists, writers and architects of the Weimar Republic looked to America with anticipation and dread as the civilisation of Europe began to crumble into violence, totalitarianism and atavism. But in 1931, they completed the Empire State building, summit of capitalist achievement and optimism. Retrospectively, we know that the Jewish world was doomed in Europe, physically destroyed by Nazism, battered by Communism. By 1925, the great wave of immigration into America had come to an end, and was henceforth to be curbed into a thin trickle. But the Jews could now crystallise some of their earlier tendencies into the shape of a community with a character of its own. The literature written up to 1934 naturally evinces the contours of this peculiar but vibrant experience. Levinsky's career in Abraham Cahan's novel spans the years 1885-1915, 'the great age of the lower East Side' (Howe), the area of greatest Jewish immigrant concentration in New York. The early major Jewish immigrant writing (in Cahan's case both Yiddish and English, moving from the former to the latter) is wrapped up with this world and its processes.

So the subject of this phase of American Jewish fiction is in the words of one critic 'the process of assimilation and the resultant crisis of identity' (Guttmann). An American Jew, conscious of being in both worlds or unconsciously trapped in ambiguity, had to ask the question that Meyer Levin (b. 1905) on reflection later posed to himself. 'Was I an American or a Jew? Could one be both?' In fact, Levin has himself suggested many of the phrases of the dialectic in his own long career, moving through a Dos Passos type realism, Proletarianism (of the type exemplified by Michael Gold), Hasidism (Jewish pietism) and Zionism. The Jewish writer not only described the Jewish world, America, things in general, but often also advocated a solution or at least a direction. This concern with the past shaping the present, self-definition within an otherwise alien world is not a characteristic exclusive to Jews. If America were uniquely neutral and absorbent of all its components in the famous melting pot, there might be no problem. But the component, in the Jewish example, has not been an ecstatic partner in its self-obliteration, and neither has the melting pot been so benignly disinterested. Ethnicity keeps breaking out.

But are these interests central to American life, and does the fiction produced constitute major literature? Certainly, Jewish fiction of the period did not catch the public imagination to the extent that did Faulkner, Hemingway, Fitzgerald, or for that matter, Jack London or Sinclair Lewis. Even the greatest works of the 'genre' such as *Call it Sleep* were soon forgotten. This might be a comment either on the quality of such work or on the marginality of its interest. Both possibilities are raised even by one of its promoters. This Jewish literature, he says 'appears in retrospect not merely to fall short of final excellence, but to remain somehow irrelevant to the main lines of development of fiction in the United States' (Fiedler). If the theme of marginality is so dominant here, then the work must by definition be peripheral. The American Jewish novel shows the Jew on the outside trying to get in (in various ways), or perhaps coming to terms with his outsider status. Can the outsider novel be central? Are not the concerns of a minority group necessarily of only limited interest to others? Fiedler argues that the obsessive thread of the American Jewish novel through the 1920s is 'the theme of inter-marriage, with its ambiguous blending of the hope of assimilation and the threat of miscegenation'. If that is so, it may not be surprising that the mainstream of American fiction has passed it by, and that the American Jewish novel is confined to a minor role in a broad panorama where the beacons shine elsewhere.

However, fortuitous and transient taste may determine the fashion of the moment, and it is undoubtedly the case that work of enormous interest and quality was underrated. The American Jewish novel might have been considered of marginal interest as a marginal phenomenon, indeed even by the Jew himself with his aspirations towards the heart of America. But is not this 'heart' in itself illusory? Who could define the 'real' America? And where do we find it? In the glitter and despair of Fitzgerald? In the ideologically expatriate Hemingway? Our literature may be going towards a definition of the Jew in the American context. But this need not be any more remote than the need for self-definition of other writers. Outsider experience could itself be characteristic. And if it is peripheral writing, then it is only peripheral in parochial terms. Because its peripheral nature derives from another additional experience. Cahan, Lewisohn, Hecht, Fuchs and Roth, some of the writers whose works are considered here have, in various ways, expanded the range of an exotic consciousness within America. And this consciousness is one that relates, however, reluctantly, to a consciousness beyond.

One of the first notable Jewish novels, *The Rise of David Levinsky* (1917) was written by the Yiddish and English language journalist, Abraham Cahan (1860-1951), founder and editor of the outstanding Yiddish newspaper, the Jewish daily *Forward*, in existence until this very day. This novel has perhaps suffered as a literary work because of its obvious value as a social document. It projects the principal themes and concerns of the Jewish immigrant to America, but also charts his movement towards assimilation, growing Americanisation, self-distancing from the home country language and people, as well as progressive modernisation in social and religious *mores*. Cahan himself emigrated to America in 1882, and was not only a Labour journalist and activist Socialist, but also one who defended Bolshevism, saying in

1922: 'There is no difference between the Socialist and Communist parties and no reason why they should be separate – at least outside Russia.' He also defended the necessity of absolute dictatorship, although by the following year he had begun to change his views (Howe). It is therefore of special interest that *The Rise of David Levinsky* is written from the point of view, not of garment manufacturer or trade unionist, but, of one risen from the ranks, an enormously successful capitalist in the newly growing (mainly now Russian-Jewish dominated) garment industry of New York.

The story is told by David Levinsky himself, reviewing his remarkable life story thirty years after his immigration. 'Sometimes, when I think of my past in a superficial, casual way, the metamorphosis I have gone through strikes me as nothing short of a miracle.' The earliest memory is of himself at three years old in Antomir when his father died. His grinding poverty is relieved by cleverness, so he succeeds at the Yeshivah (talmudical academy). Although perspicacious and pious, he displays erotic awareness early (at the age of 14) and a few years later begins to question the basic assumptions of his environment. At the age of 18 he is attacked on Easter Day, and when his mother tries to intervene she is killed. This is a commonplace enough occurrence of the time; through poverty and legal deprivation, subjection to arbitrary mob violence. Now an orphan, David is the object of charity, so he can 'eat days' (i.e. receive free meals) with Reb Sender. Impelled both by his own circumstances and outside questioning, he doubts divine providence and feels alienated from Antomir. The events of spring 1881 brought about a transformation of sentiment. 'Over five million people were suddenly made to realise that their birthplace was not their home (a feeling which the great Russian revolution had suddenly changed).' The new concrete factor is the possibility of emigration to America, and he receives the necessary assistance from a more assimilated lady benefactor.

In much immigrant literature, the fact of immigration transcends the mere episodic and assumes a larger dimension of being created anew. The subject is born again. 'The immigrant's arrival in his new home is like a second birth to him. Imagine a new-born babe in possession of a fully developed intellect. Would it ever forget its entry into the world? Neither does the immigrant ever forget his entry into a country, which is, to him, a new world in the profoundest sense of the term and in which he expects to pass the rest of his life.' In 1885, there was no restriction on immigration, so the newcomer could arrive without means, without contacts, without skills or trade, without English.

Much of the account of the newly-arrived David is of his transition from greenhorn to American, and the stages in the process are both an account of acclimatisation and of inconspicuous assimilation. It was a society worth cultivating, because in the USA even the poverty indicated greater prosperity than in the Pale of Settlement. Correspondingly, everything was different here — even the orthodox Jew was relatively assimilated. Here are some features: everyone was known by his Gentile name; no-one slept in the synagogue; Jews did not pray so regularly; they all went out to work of some sort (it was a growing economy); males, on the whole, did not wear sidelocks; women were not segregated; they all adopted a Western style of dress. These things may seem superficial, but Levinsky made the personal discovery that 'if orthodoxy bends, it breaks': 'The very clothes I wore and the very food I ate had a fatal effect on my religious habits. A whole book could be written on the influence of a starched collar and a necktie on a man who was brought up as I was.'

From the external transformation to the internal realisation is a long journey for Levinsky. He is essentially naive at the time described, and does not indulge in great analysis of his own processes. He is now an American, a secularist, a philanderer. He speaks English fluently. He notes that the Jews from Russia in their local adaptation had become atheists, whereas those from Germany had tended rather to modify their religion. So much for the sociology of the immigrant and his metaphysical stance. A great deal of the following is occupied with an account of Levinsky's business success and, incidentally, a description of the garment industry and its transformation at that time. There is a great deal of circumstantial detail retailed in the description of how Levinsky got established, acquiring credit, selling shirts on the basis of samples, and setting up in mass production. But this is perhaps a fault of the novel which, although gripping, partly reads like social history, and is written in the meagre language of that discipline.

The narrative persona in the novel is politically opposed to Cahan's own. Levinsky adopts the ideological stance of a Spencerian Darwinist, advocating the survival of the fittest. His success proves his worth; that he has adapted shows that he should be selected. But with the passage of time, he begins to feel dissatisfaction and loneliness. At the age of forty, he not only decides that he should start a family but he also then hankers after his ancestral traditions. He contemplates marriage into the orthodox establishment: 'While free from any vestige of religion in the ordinary meaning of the word, I was tingling with a religious ecstasy that was based on a sense of public duty.' There is also something fervent in his Americanism and in the observed loyalty of fellow Jews: 'It was as if they were saying, "we are not persecuted under this flag. At last we have found a home."' The projected marriage does not come off, but this question of 'who are you living for' continues to nag away. He surveys his life and achievements in ultimate dissatisfaction: 'The gloomiest past is dearer than the brightest present.' He goes beyond nostalgia to a sense of ultimate failure and dislocation. Then he concludes: 'I can never forget the days of my misery. I cannot escape from my old self. My past and present do not comport well. David, the poor lad swinging over a Talmud volume at the Preacher's Synagogue, seems to have more in common with my inner identity than David Levinsky, the well-known cloak manufacturer.'

We can chart the stages of Levinsky's apostasy — getting bored with the Talmud, his friend Naphtali's declared heresy, his mother's death (removing the anchor and the rudder), staying with a Russified family and particularly falling under the influence of the daughter Matilda, his first love, emigration and the need to adapt. There are further stages to the process in America — dressing in a modern way, shaving off his beard, business, success and ideological Darwinism, eroticism. But ultimately, the novel is not really of a piece, suddenly veering (with his own middle age) in a different direction, and expressing dissatisfaction with all his manifold achievements and earlier aspirations. Of course, people change in the course of their development. But here the ground is not previously prepared for the later sense of failure, loneliness and ultimate nostalgia. Clearly, the character is split. But we do not fully understand, for example, why Levinsky does not go through with his marriage. The novel moves off in too many different directions. Clearly, the narrator does not wholly grasp his own nature. The trouble is that the author and narrator here are too intermingled. The author does not step out of the skin of the narrator to transmit, whether implicitly or explicitly, any understanding through a wider lens, by which Levinsky's character and development could be grasped in context. The novel is fascinating and rich in detail, with great insights and peaks, but not ultimately satisfying in its conspectus.

Most intellectual of the novelists discussed here is Ludwig Lewisohn (1882-1955), whose work is both more rooted in a European tradition and more theoretical as well as more programmatic in intent. In *The Island Within* (1928), the author not only presents part of a family chronicle in relation to the Levys, but also a view of the Jew in America

against a broader backdrop of Jewish history. He refuses to consider
the American Jew in isolation, either from America, or from Jews
elsewhere. It is very much a part of the general Jewish story, however
much people have deluded themselves to the contrary view. Lewisohn
insists, in one of a series of prologues which precede each section, that
the novel has to recapture an epic quality: 'To do that there is no need
of high-flown words or violent actions. Only a constant sense of the
streaming generations, of the processes of historic change, of the true
character of man's magnificent and tragic adventure between earth and
sky.'

In this sense, *The Island Within* is a roman-à-thèse, but one genuinely
felt. The story opens in the Vilna of 1840, with Mendel and his wife
Braine. For East European Jewry, this is the early phase of that period
in Jewish history styled the 'Haskalah', Enlightenment, and Mendel,
much to his pious wife's distress, catches this bug. Mendel remains
within the fold, but his son Efraim becomes even more secular, and
goes to Prussia as Efraim Levy in 1850. Through his use of prologues
(à la *Tom Jones*), the author gives the reader both the story and his
reflection on the events. In recent history particularly, but throughout
the generations, Jews have had to migrate. For him, this is a negative
phenomenon: 'The Jews are not the only migratory folk of modern
times, but they furnish the classic examples of migration, because
nowhere have they yet found the rest of either tolerance or land.' If the
principal overt subject of the novel is the Jew in America, the larger
question is whether the Jew is at home anywhere on the globe. Efraim
is happy to be in Prussia, but that country is still for him an exile
(goles). His son, Tobias, asserts that he is genuinely at home. but he has
to prove himself as a German, so he fights in the Franco-Prussian war of
1870, is awarded the iron cross for bravery, marries a Christian,
changing his name to hers, and then gets baptised. Altogether, as a well-
married senior lawyer, he enjoys great financial and social success.
What an irony: 'all literary and artistic Berlin crowded their drawing-
rooms. Almost all were Jews.' Is he properly assimilated now? No,
because he is troubled by other memories. He hopes that his children
might be free of such.

But it is principally another branch of the family whose fortunes
we follow. Tobias's young brother Jacob escapes military service and
goes to America, saying: 'We are treated like dogs here, I want to go to a
free country.' He becomes thoroughly Americanised, paradoxically by
being much more German than he had ever been back in Insterburg.
According to all reasonable expectations, this should signify the end

of the Jewish chapter in this story of the generations. But somehow, through all the disguises and the obliqueness, the children always knew that they were Jewish. Arthur, whose story occupies most of the book, early protests that there is no Jewish problem. Again, war acts as a litmus test of national loyalty, and Arthur pronounces himself ready to conscript in the event of American involvement in the Great War. It does not come to that in his case. He qualifies as a doctor in 1918, turns to psychiatry and then to psychoanalysis, then marries Elizabeth Knight, a feminist journalist. After committing himself thus to a neutral American affiliation, he discovers his own separateness in his attitude to family, particularly to his son, to his past and to America. America was becoming more segmented and Jews more sectioned off and delimited rather than less. Nearly all his patients were Jews: 'He found that their physical aches and inhibitions and discomforts were all flights from an obscure reality.' And the reason is, he holds, that they are not really at home. The Jew had no Gentile hearthstone, 'no centre to which to retire'. Through the eyes of his wife he can discern the Jew's alienation more clearly, and he 'knew suddenly why Jews were sometimes physically unmannerly. On different ground, emotionally out of touch, aiming wildly, one aims amiss.' The question asks not only where the Jew is placed socially, but where he is placed emotionally. Elizabeth is prepared to accept circumcision for their son, but it is quite a different matter for Arthur who sees is as a commitment to the Jewish people. The social ostracism which Arthur witnesses *vis-à-vis* both himself and others (towards his sister Hazel, who had been an ideological assimilator, for example) forces him to turn inwards, and makes him, albeit reluctantly, consider divorce: 'We're fond of each other and we understand each other intellectually, but at the emotional basis of life there is no, no opposition – there's a divergence', he says to his brother-in-law.

The problem that Lewisohn sets before us in Arthur's story is of an ideal trapped in self-delusion. Arthur, like other Jews, had tried to live like an American Protestant without being one: 'And so we live in a void, in a spiritual vacuum. The devil of it is we don't know exactly what we are.' The illusion is that one can be human in isolation. But Arthur now holds that you cannot be just human, but you must be a particular kind of human. He asks his wife if he is an American and, although she quickly corrects herself, her immediate answer is negative. The Jew is wanting to be American must also aspire to being Gentile. Jews have a 'gentile fixation'. It is 'the problem of the social isolation of Jews who didn't want to be Jews'. Arthur's solution is to return to accept the Jewishness that is otherwise thrust on him as a burden. In a rather contrived conclusion, he is given a family paper relating an account of an ancestor's martyrdom during Godfrey's crusade. Even then, the Jew's search for security, his failure to establish it, his plight and eventual martyrdom, established for Arthur that what the Jew was really looking for was 'a home in the homeless world'. And if the Jew has not got a physical home, at least he has an anchor in an idea: 'For if history has an ethical direction its symbol is not the clansmen or the warrior, but he who passively defends an idea and thus sanctifies an ineffable Name.' Thus the world can be rendered home once more and be a 'natural habitation'.

There were other notions proposed as to how to resolve man's (but more particularly the Jew's) homelessness. The understanding that the unit belonged to a larger mass would deny this troublesome individualism. And literature could take its place too as a handmaiden to the new society. Such was the nature of totalitarian Communism and the absolutist view of literature that emerged within the Soviet Union, adopted also by a coterie of those enlightened outside. This view achieved its ultimate expression at the Soviet Writer's Congress of 1934, when Socialist Realism was articulated as an ideal. The writer has a supportive role within a Communist framework. He is, in Stalin's words, 'an engineer of the human soul'. Andrey Zhdanov, Secretary of the Central Committee of the Communist Party of the Soviet Union, formulated the writer's task as 'knowing life so as to be able to depict it truthfully in works of art, not to depict it in a dead, scholastic way, not simply as "objective reality", but to depict reality in its revolutionary development' (Scott). He then issued instructions to the writers present: 'Create works of high attainment, of high ideological and artistic content. Actively help to remould the mentality of people in the spirit of socialism.'

Such doctrines (here formulated in 1934 but enforced much earlier) had their adherents in the USA too. Remarkably, given Soviet attitudes to Jews and Judaism which were to be fully manifest later but were already latent, many American Communists and even Stalinists were of Jewish origin. Michael Gold (1896-1967) set out to be a proletarian writer. As he writes in *120 Million* (1929), he had felt lonely and was now bolstered by the mass (the number of the title refers to the American population): 'Mass is strength, mass is clarity and courage.' He has passed from the traditional isolation of the writer to expression of the group: 'From ego-poet to mass-poet is the usual path of the proletarian writer.' And now he self-identifies with the Soviet Union, which is the source of his strength: 'Poetry,' he asserts 'is used in Soviet Russia as a means of welding the masses into solidarity.' Like the poets there, he would say that poetry should be useful, and write 'workers' chants'. He pleads for revolution in America, invoking Lenin and the 'bloody birth that he will bring':

'I see a Hammer-Sun by day,
A Sickle-Moon by night.
Shining on a new America,
A Workers' and Farmers' America.'

As demanded by the Zhdanov Imperative, Gold scorns objectivity, and invests his observations with pathos. In his description of miners: 'They shuffled in the morning through the muddy streets toward the mine pit, and returned in the dusk with their emptied dinner pails, their faces black as sinister masks, their bodies dripping sweat, and stopped in weary curves'. There was no God of justice, for there was no justice, only pain and futility. In a merciless world, the employers are corrupt and police violent. The proletarian leader must suffer because 'a new world was being born out of his agonies'.

It is here that we have the other side of the hopeful immigration. Here, everything has gone wrong and there is no hope for the future: 'He had entered the factories a hopeful immigrant, with youthful, rosy cheeks that he had brought from Russia, and a marvellous faith in the miracle of the Promised Land that also emanated from there. The sweatshops had soon robbed him of that youthful bloom, however; then they had eaten slowly, like a beast in a cave gnawing for days at a carcass, his lungs, his stomach, his heart, all his vital organs, one by one.' This figure is the very antithesis of Levinsky. He contrasts famine in America with famine in the Soviet Union. The latter he assures us, will come to an end, the former will persist and be multiplied into further famines. There is no plan in America for redemption (amelioration), and the capitalist world is a prison full of gratuitous violence.

For all the absurd over-simplifications, misconceptions and false prognostications, there is a certain power in the rhetoric. A more specific portrait emerges in the first-person account, *Jews without Money* (1930). This book comprises childhood memories of the East Side, not more than a block away from the Bowery. The child was already familiar with every possible social evil induced by extreme poverty. He relates of suffering and of the hypocrisy of wealth combined with bourgeois morality. He meets anti-Semitism everywhere in New York. For Gold, America represents the very opposite pole to the pilgrim dream. Its great city is a very hell on earth: 'New York is a devil's dream, the most urbanised city in the world. It is all geometry, angles and stone. It is mythical, a city buried by a volcano. No grass is found in this petrified city, no big living trees, no flowers, no bird but the drab little lecherous sparrow, no soil, loam, earth.' It is true that America has become rich, but only 'because it has eaten the tragedy of millions of immigrants'. Although Gold's perspective is very different from Cahan's in *Levinsky*, we note similar observations on the character of assimilation. The most immediate sign is change of clothing style: 'Our Sam no longer wore a fur cap, a long Jewish coat and peasant boots. No. He wore a fine gentleman's suit, a white collar like a doctor, store shoes and a beautiful round fur-hat called a derby.' There emerges a vivid picture of daily life, the poverty and the violence, the excitement, the bustle, the break from routine (a visit to Bronx park, so exciting for the townies). And there is also a personal note in his description of his mother on whom he bases his current predilections: 'Momma! Momma! I am still bound to you by the cord of birth. I cannot forget you. I must remain faithful to the poor because I cannot be faithless to you.'

The book is deliberately episodic, flitting from scene to scene to build up the general picture. Religion is seen negatively, ritual petty and irritating, in fact, neurotic: 'Religion was a fervent affair on the East Side. Every persecuted race becomes a race of fanatics.' But the one Jewish concept to which the author is sympathetic is the Messianic idea. And that is because the Messiah will effect revolutionary change and not leave the world in its present unredeemed state. The Messiah is brought into current history in the Marxist sense, and secularised. The Messiah is the revolution. 'O workers' Revolution, you brought home to me, a lonely suicidal boy. You are the true Messiah.' This Messiah could redeem humanity from the humiliation of job-seeking on a seller's market, from gang warfare in which the strongest, most vindictive and ruthless always win out, from perpetual poverty and human degradation. The world could and eventually (in Gold's view) would be transformed into the workers' paradise that the Soviet Union was becoming, with the people's dictator at the helm of State. Needless to say too, in such a world there will be no division between Jews and Gentile, or indeed between any races since this division, like war and conflict generally, is created by the cruelty involved in capitalism. What Gold shows us as Judaism is a transient phase in progress towards the revolution that will obliterate ethnic or religious separatism as obscurantist and divisive.

The style of Ben Hecht (1894-1964) is as different from Gold's as can be imagined. His writing, concerned with the world of current affairs and journalism, is not Jew-centred. But in the one novel of his, *A Jew in Love* (1931) where he does ponder the nature of the Jew, his writing is unrhetorical, literate, subtle and baroque. The novel describes one Jo Boshere and, in particular, as indicated by the title, his erotic adventures. But these amorous practices are not divorced from his Jewish nature and complexes. On the contrary, they express them, both in his flight from Judaism and in his nostalgia for it. Hecht begins his story with a long introductory description of the hero before any action actually takes place. And the hero Boshere is unmistakably and invincibly Jewish: 'Boshere was no matter for wincing, yet he had an uncomfortably Semitic face, a face stamped with the hieroglyphic curl of the Hebrew alphabet.' With his fate in his countenance, he must learn to accept it. Boshere, at the opening of the book, is already mature and successful. So the book, unlike *Levinsky*, is not a description of a man's rise. The novel's subject is rather the man's nature and its particular expression in erotic outlet, what it means to be a Jew in love.

Jo Boshere (born Abe Nussbaum, his change of name indicating the need for assimilation and acceptability) is already married when we meet him. But his marriage is of a very peculiar sort. No sooner does this marriage take place than Boshere arranges that they should always be apart, making sure that she keeps going on long trips. What led him to her in the first place? Perhaps he was attracted to her concern for him: 'her chief resemblance to Boshere was her almost insane preoccupation with him'. Boshere is totally selfish, blind to the needs of others. In fact, his main ambition is to incorporate these others into his own rampant ego: 'Although he began each of his wooings with passionate, rapist pretenses, his ardor in this direction was no more than a mask for his real purpose which was that of a deeper and more inner seduction, a Dracula-like hunger for the life blood of his victim.' He cannot tolerate separate, autonomous individuals — only satellites around himself. But his Jewishness remains his problem. He at first tries to transcend it. But then Tillie Marmon, the object of his most constant desire, makes it clear that it is precisely this Jewish element that appeals to her in its foreignness: 'His Jewishness had become for her an exotic mask, mysterious and oriental ... The process of changing from Jew to Oriental, from an anti-Semitic cartoon to a glamorous illustration out of the Arabian Nights, worked a spell on Boshere. He felt grateful.' This external perception of him helps him to revise his own estimate of his Jewish character. But he wants to use his Jewish nature and characteristics for display, to stand above them in control as a sophisticated cosmopolitan who can turn on his origins at will, and scorns hiding them. But, as indicated by relations with his family, particularly with his sister Esther, he does not want to be swamped by this Jewishness. He is especially nervous of Esther's Zionist associations. Perhaps this is because Zionism implies total assent to Jewishness. Esther tells him: '"You're ashamed to have associated with the Jewish cause because it reflects on you. It reminds people that you're a Jew".' For him though, Zionism is self-deception, a pretence that 'now Jews are respectable'.

It would seem from a superficial reading of the novel that its concern is not with the 'Jew' part of the title, but rather with the 'love' part of it. But what is the nature of Jo's 'love'? Is it, in fact, love at all, or is there not perhaps an irony in the title? Love, if it means anything, requires profound concern with the other, the object of such love. The lover should lose himself in an altruistic giving. But Jo seems unable to give, and is eternally beset not by concern for the partner (on the contrary, he can flit from one to another and deceive all without a qualm), but by his own insecurity. Do they really 'love' him is what he wants to know. Are they constantly, tightly wrapped up in his being? In fact, when he suspects that he has genuinely fallen in love, he perceives that as a humiliation. Of course, the person loving is less in control than the object of love, and what Jo seeks above all is control. Control is power: 'Love itself was valueless to his egosim. To love another in fact was a queer and unbearable rivalry. He felt angered and belittled by it. His chief concern, touched by the lure of another, had been to arouse immediate and overwhelming love in this other.' But just as his love is inauthentic, so is his Jewishness. 'A Jew in love' is only a self-conscious, parodic description of his own activity. Hecht indeed hardly lets the action speak for itself. The plot does not emerge to the reader's interpretation. On the contrary, the reader is given Jo's thoughts and the omniscient narrator's view of the thought and its framework. But because the chief character has not achieved maturity and self-understanding, he can never grow beyond the datum of narcissism. This can look either funny or terrible to the outsider, so the tone of this attractive narrative veers between farce and tragedy. If 'love' is the principal subject then it is inauthentic love emanating from an inauthentic Jew. Jo has not grappled with his essential nature in any respect. He has fulfilled himself in society for society, but not for himself in his true essence. Certainly not as a Jew.

One of the exciting things about this literature is the way that it is being rediscovered after the years of oblivion following publication. Daniel Fuchs (b.1909), in his 1961 preface to the published three novels, writes of their immediate obscurity. We now see that the work is brilliant. But the writer did not understand what he was doing. '*Summer in Williamsburg* (1934) was written in a state of sheer terror,' he says. A panorama of life in this New York suburb, funny and tragic, was written like a diary: 'I was determined to write fairly. I wanted to examine everything with an absolutely clear view, unencumbered and unaffected.' He composed it out of 'ignorance or innocence'. And it comes over to us as a mixture of naturalism and fantasy, raised to a level of major creative fiction. Like Gold, Fuchs sets his work in the heart of the Jewish proletariat. But the representation is comic and sympathetic.

As this novel moves about so much from person to person and from scene to scene, it is difficult to speak of a single hero or of an overall plot. A central action does emerge in the warfare between two gangs, each of which wants to set up an interurban bus company and put the other out of business. The gang with which we get better acquainted, under the leadership of Papravel, wins out in the end. And the hero? Perhaps this is Williamsburg itself with all its characters. There are scenes of violence and puzzlement. The young Philip Hayman is more than any other the lens, the detached observer, of his father: 'He's old and Momma's worn and Harry's on his way, already a stranger, while I, of course, move along the moonlit paths like a moving picture star untouched by life, detached and above.' There is a wealth of character, a human comedy. Philip, unable to commit himself either to love or to life, sees himself as a movie hero. A movie hero, of course, only has a limited reality, controllable and glamorous, from which the character can be detached and remain ultimately untouched. And so Williamsburg, for him, is a film set. Adult gang warfare is paralleled by fights amongst groups of children. In case we do not take the story sufficiently seriously, death keeps intervening. Everyone, for example, knows that Mr Miller is dying, but no-one knows of what. He echoes the point made in Tolstoy's story 'The Death of Ivan Ilyich' that death is something expected for others. 'A man is born, he grows and grows, and dies. We must expect that, everyone says, but we who say it never do. We expect death in others, to ourselves it is always remote and impossible.' Philip remains on the fringes of society, asked by his brother Harry to join Papravel's gang, by Tessie for love, by his father to return to the bosom of his family. He is wanted by all, and sympathetic to all. But he still hovers in his created movie dream. Other people commit themselves — Cohen to politics, Harry to crime, his father to charity. But all these, one way or another, retract their commitment. Cohen is not a genuine communist. Harry leaves Papravel just at the point when he has won out over his rival, Morand, and the father, suffering his squalor, also has doubts over his life of altruism.

The author has difficulty in finding an appropriate focus. God is introduced rather facetiously at the end: 'And now He peers down, and for a moment His gaze rests again on Williamsburg and He says to Himself, how are things going on down there, I wonder ... God wonders and looks. Everything is just as it has always been and as it will be.' This is an ending that does not conclude. God is as indecisive as the characters on and off the set, and the plot is circular rather than linear. As in his later novel, *Homage to Blenholt* (1936), where the setting is the same though the characters different, we are entertained and saddened by the passing scene which moves round and round rather than on and in sequence. We are not working the thing out here or coming to a denouement. There is just observation.

The most striking work of the genre is undoubtedly *Call it Sleep* (1934) by Henry Roth (b.1906), his only novel. It is unusual not only in its potency but in its single focus. All is seen, apart from the prologue which puts the chief figure in context, through the eyes of the six-to-seven-year-old child, David Schearl. The advantage of this focus lies in the natural perception of subtleties in relationship through the heightened sensitivity of a child. And yet although the account is filtered through the child, the reader is made aware by implication of things that only an adult could comprehend. The child struggles for meaning in order to make sense of his own environment, of this strange, hostile world, of brutish America, of overbearing father, of arrogant, over-confident children, of the very threat of things in themselves. Although the story is told in the third person and David is introduced as one of the characters, all the others are seen in relation to him and usually spoken of in terms of that relationship, e.g. David's father, David's mother, etc.

David has come to America as a young child (precisely how old he was is one of the open points on which turns the question of paternity), and the story is then picked up several years later. As the infant could not have a sufficiently accurate and broad perception to register the impact of immigration, this is conveyed from the outside. He is brought by his mother to rejoin his father who has already settled in the New

World. His mother ironically cries: '"And this is the Golden Land"' after we read of 'the stench and throb of the steerage to the stench and throb of New York tenements'. The relationships — David/mother/ father/Land — are immediately established. The father is extraordinarily hostile to both the other members of the family, especially in view of the fact that they have just arrived. Of the child he says: '"He's the cause of all the trouble anyway."' The environment in return is hostile to David, as represented, for example, by the water tap. 'Standing before the kitchen sink and regarding the bright faucets that gleamed so far away, each with a bead of water at its nose, slowly swelling, falling, David again became aware that this world had been created without thought of him.' Although the child's vision is manifest, the range of observation is made credible. Ther is a unity of language. The language implied when the parents are talking is Yiddish, conveyed in normative, rich English. But when the immigrants go over to English (for outsiders, or the children amongst themselves), they speak dialect. None of them are really at home here.

The triangular relationship of father/mother/son has its parallel with Lawrence's *Sons and Lovers*, in the hostility of the father and the protectiveness of the mother *vis-à-vis* the child. The father, inarticulate and violent, feels an outsider, and mother only seems to care deeply for the son, although she is willing to carry out her wifely duties. The son has to find refuge from the constant terror of the world in the mother. The father is out of his depth in this urban construct: '"When you come out of a house and step on the bare earth among the fields you're the same man you were when you were inside the house. But when you step on pavements, you're someone else. You can feel your face change."' It is the father's face changed that we see in his house. Everyone fears his violence and unpredictability. But it is not only his father who frightens David. The other children in the tenement block seem to know things that are slightly out of David's reach. The crippled Annie tries to initiate David into the 'bad', i.e. sex. This is so terrifying: 'But she [i.e. his mother] didn't know as he knew how the whole world could break into a thousand little pieces, all buzzing, all whining, and no-one hearing them and no-one seeing them except himself.' David's world is now fragmented. Everywhere is threat — the guest Luter who comes frequently to the house and whom he perceives dimly as a rival for his mother's attention, the policemen who do not seem to be able to help him find his way home when he gets lost, the streets which, beyond his own, are unfamiliar (he does not even know the name of his own street accurately). 'Everything he knew frightened him.'

We only have the workings of David's consciousness. Everyone else is recorded by David, so the reader can only observe them from the outside too, by their actions and speech. The family moves from Brownsville to the lower East Side so that the father can be nearer his work as a milkman (after the accident, he was rendered incapable of working in a printing press). This is 'a new and violent world'. But there is a new mediator in the shape of Aunt Bertha, his mother's sister newly arrived. Extrovert, unafraid, although not presentable and with scanty knowledge of English, she can introduce David more into a realm beyond the family home. She possesses secret information about his mother and her relations with a certain 'organist' back in the old country. Through half-understood bits of recollections and confidences, David gathers that she had known this organist very intimately, but that as he was already engaged, he was not available to her (as well as being non-Jewish of course). She had seen him for a last time in a field of corn (of particular significance, since one of the few things she bought for the New York apartment was a painting of a cornfield). Six months later, she had met Albert and quickly married him. There seems to be a mystery here too, as the world is permeated by mysteries. But those which involve his mother are of particular concern to David. Another mystery is God, about whom he begins to learn at cheder (Hebrew school). They read Isaiah's vision of the Lord seated on His throne, and David is determined to locate this formidable phenomenon. He, through enigmatic hints, learns to associate God with a very bright light, 'brighter than the day is brighter than night'. So David sees God as sunlight on water, and then more vividly, by throwing a zinc sword on the railtrack, when 'light, unleashed, terrific light bellowed out of iron lips'. His cheder teacher disputes this view of God, but David is unconvinced by such disparagement.

New territories invade David's own. There is Leo Dukovka, of Polish origin, so free, exciting and independent. There are his cousins Esther and Polly, revelling in a sexuality that is disgusting to the child. Through a complicated sequence of events, the story of his mother's previous association leaks out to the father who now has all his instinctive suspicions confirmed: '"All these years my blood told me! Whispered to me whenever I looked at him, nudged me, told me he wasn't mine."' And when he goes to whip him, a rosary (given by Leo) falls out of the child's pocket. This confirms it all. It is '"a sign, a witness"'. At this point David runs out again to the railtrack. To have his vision vouchsafed once more? In achieving this blinding light, a 'roaring radiance, candescent', this time his foot gets burned. After being ripped by five hundred and fifty volts, his escape can be regarded as a resurrection. As he truthfully says to his mother, he does not know why he went to the tracks. Now to overcome the terror of life he can only sleep. Sleep can strike a spark in the darkness. So whether it is actually sleep or not (as suggested by his mother's question), 'he might as well call it sleep'. There is a catharsis at the novel's end. The terror has been encountered at source. David has actually been in the presence of this God, fully met all His dangers and emerged alive. The security issuing from his mother's reality has come through to the child against the power of God and all the other dark and hostile forces. This is the one fixed point in the child's world. In the alien street, for example, he would sometimes see her unexpectedly: 'Catching sight of her accidentally this way always gave him an intense thrill of pleasure. It was as though the street's shifting intricacy had flowered into the simple steadiness of her presence, as though days not hours had passed since he had seen her because days not hours had passed since he had seen her in the street.' The mysterious comfort of sleep at the end of the book is associated with the comfort of his mother against the terrifying source of power in the track. That power is the enemy. Perhaps after this achievement of peace, the child will have attained the maturity to cope. *Call it Sleep* is the rendition of a childhood world of terror overcome in crisis. It is a very special, but, of its nature, unrepeatable work.

3 A BRIEF SPRING: IN THE GERMAN WORLD BETWEEN THE WARS

It is well known that the Jews in the German-speaking world in the early years of this century played a part in those regions disproportionate to their relatively low representation. Until the declaration of what has been called the 'war against the Jews' (Davidowicz), epitomised by Hitler's assumption of the chancellorship in 1933, the Jews constituted no more than about one per cent of the population of Germany proper, i.e. about half a million. In Vienna, although not elsewhere in Austria, there was a greater concentration of Jewry that was boosted by a wave of emigration from the East in the wake of the Great War. Jewish population reached about 170,000 in that great city. And in Czechoslovakia, there were about 200,000, evenly divided between what Hitler took as the 'Protectorate' (Bohemia and Moravia) in March 1939 (what was to be a joint, autonomous part of the Reich) and Slovakia.

We have already noted the rise of anti-Semitism in Germany/Austria in the late nineteenth century. And yet there seemed to emerge an astonishing degree of cultural efflorescence between Jews and Germans at a later stage; a dream become nightmare by the 1930s and 1940s. Cultural historians have remarked the Jewish contribution in particular fields: 'There was the strong Jewish element, as so often in the forefront of avant-gardism. But the role of the Jews in the visual arts was minute' (Laqueur). This apparent (illusory or temporary?) renaissance proceeded, as is now so painfully obvious, amidst rejection and alienation. We can never be quite certain as to why a particular concatenation took place, and any speculation is based on the wisdom of hindsight. The Jews of the late nineteenth and early twentieth centuries bridged two cultures — the one from which they were emerging and the one to which they were aspirant. The first seemed coercive and restrictive, the second appealing and challenging. It may have been the vigour of the response propelled by the discipline and historical shape of the background that made the master of the new universe possible.

Everything following the Great War seemed to be in flux. Political borders, assumptions about war, which had hitherto been an exercise limited to the professionals and the unfortunate but now affected everyone, and even human nature itself. Art and human philosophy had to accommodate the changed spectrum of experience. No country exemplified this difference more vividly than did Germany. She had lost a war, an Empire and a Kaiser, and with them all an assumption about her own grandeur. Then she did not take easily to republicanism. Extreme interpretations of defeat were followed by extremist remedies. Revolutionary burgeonings, such as that of the Spartacists led by Rosa Luxemburg amongst others, were followed by bouts of continuing violence (Luxemburg herself was murdered in January 1919). The Treaty of Versailles was one-sided and presented non-negotiable demands based on the assumption of exclusive German guilt. This generated, fuelled and justified a nationalist revanchism. Growing anti-Semitism was one aspect of the anti-republican sentiment. In fact Jews were not prominent in German politics, obviously not on the right but not on the far left either. The most prominent one, industrialist turned foreign minister Walter Rathenau, was assassinated in the attempted putsch of 1922. This came at the height of the hyper-inflation. Miraculously the mark was suddenly stabilised at the end of 1923, which was followed by the 'golden years' of the Republic, 1924 to 1929, when the collapse of Wall Street forced America to withdraw its backing from the Republic. Thereupon followed the well-known disintegration (McKenzie). The embrace of a terrifying dictatorship had a psychological resonance, but also a suitable economic and political backdrop.

So Germany and the German-speaking world enjoyed an exhilirating if brief splendour. 'But it was a precarious glory, a dance on the edge of a volcano. Weimar culture was the creation of outsiders, propelled by history into the inside, for a short, dizzying, fragile moment' (Gay). The historians of the period experience the usual difficulties of definition. The characteristic elements of 'Weimar culture' were already manifest before the war. 'Expressionism', for example, was a term that had already been coined by Wilhelm Worringer in 1911 to characterise the new fashions in literature. But it was broadened to cover a wide range of art form, that mainly associated with the horrors of world war, mass man, the universalisation of particular experience and modern technology. Architecture (the Bauhaus school), painting (such as Beckmann's), theatre (Frank Wedekind, who already flourished in the late nineteenth century, and also Bertholt Brecht), poetry (Gottfried Benn), the novel (Thomas Mann had already produced major works in the first decade of the century) indicated new perspectives. The Jewish writer could only painfully readjust his perspective, carrying what seemed to be a dead past. Politics drifted away from culture.

There was a 'lack of connection between culture and politics in Weimar, and of influence by intellectuals on polity' (Laqueur).

What we will look at here is not the whole range of Jewish expression in this context. That would be enormously complicated, difficult to disentangle, and inevitably nit-picking. But within this confused, exciting world some searchlights were beamed that sought to combine a historical sense with the ethnic self-identification of Fate; these together with the selection of a path through the contemporary world. Voices of puzzlement and attempted interpretation were heard. Prophets, guides, or simply echoes of current bewilderment. Some writers, theologians and critics found new ways of describing the experience of man perplexed fleeing anonymous judgement in the attempt at self-justification, of man in the universe *vis-à-vis* God and History, society and self.

Franz Kafka (1883-1924), whose writings loom larger than ever with every successive year, also remains as enigmatic as ever. His three novels were not only unpublished (except for small extracts) within his lifetime, but were also unfinished. And a Kafka novel is unfinishable in principle, even though the author would like to introduce a resolution. This is the nature of the labyrinth.

Many are the interpretations of Kafka's work. Comic, hopeless, ambitious, his figures move either on or round and round in a smoke-filled world. The light may occasionally seem to filter through, but then it might be illusory. The Kafka character is concerned with the search and the path (in the religious sense too). But we as readers never can be assured that this search is taking place and path being walked in the traditional understanding of religious direction. If a trial is held, there must be judges and a law certainly. But is there a quality of abstract justice, and can the man judged ever know the law by which he is being judged? There is evidently a 'castle', but can K ever reach the authority behind it? Even 'America', the land of opportunities described in Kafka's happiest work, is not totally unravelled.

The novels and tales sound rather more like parables than modern fiction. And the author has adopted the traditional literary mode of the parable (mashal) with its canons and authorial anonymity. The 'wise man' speaks. The world projected also looks like the old world of certainties, when God reigned supreme, and man's function was to anticipate the divine will and act in accordance with it. 'The Parables' tell us about faith in the Emperor. But, on the other hand, this may be the faith pinned on an enigmatic anchor in a sea of confusion: 'Pekin

itself is far stranger to the people in our village than the next world.'
This does not mean that the Law may be abrogated. On the contrary,
it is sacrosanct in every particular. But it is only recorded in the ancient
texts, and there is no live understanding of it. 'Our life,' it is noted
'...is subject to no contemporary law, and attends only to the
exhortations and warnings which come to us from olden times.' And
paradoxically, it is just this tentative connection which 'should seem
to be (zu sein scheint) one of the greatest unifying influences among
our people ... the very ground on which we live'. The authority of the
past, however obscure, arbitrary or peculiar, is the only solid basis
for present existence.

There are two ways of looking at Kafka's work. The author himself,
in a letter to his fiancée Felice (whom, of course, he never married)
wrote: 'I have no literary interest, but am made of literature. I am
nothing else and cannot be anything else' (14 August 1913). As in
his famous story (so particularly valued, even by himself) 'The Hunger
Artist', he saw an ultimately preclusive contrast between literature
and life. In his diary entry of the same period, he wrote about Felice,
'I cannot live without her, nor with her' (12, 13 May 1913). He could
neither marry nor not marry. If he was not writing he felt impotent,
and if he was writing he became totally possessed. He was literally in
his own eyes unfit for living, and only fit for literature. His close friend,
executor and biographer, however, in a judgement upon him writes:
'The category of sacredness (and not really that of literature) is the
only right category under which Kafka's life and work can be viewed'
(Brod). In this view, Kafka is not producing aesthetic material, but a
sort of holy text. What he wrote had to be judged as truth, not as
adornment or pleasurable experience.

The theme of judgement pervades Kafka's writing. But it is an odd
sort of judgement in which the guilt is never to be doubted. As in the
story 'In the Penal Colony', where the condemned man does not
know why the sentence is passed, nor even what the sentence is. And
there is certainly no opportunity for defence. A critic has written:
'The Law without a lawgiver, original sin without a god to disobey; this
is the essence of the negative theology that pervades Kafka's stories and
novels. Their protagonists are sinful almost *because* there is no God to
sin against, guilty almost because there is no Sinai, for although there is
no God and no lawgiver, their souls are cast in the mould in which
the fear of God and the obedience to His law is inscribed. It is a
situation in which sin and guilt, more often than not, appear to lie not
in any *doing* but in *being*, in being a separate individual' (Heller).

Heller characterises the Kafka world as a totality of perfection and unity in which man has sinned by breaking away into individual life. Enlightenment, which is to say, knowledge of the source of Law, might be achieved, but only (as in this story) at the moment of death. Brod tries to bring Kafka more down to earth, to the world of political reality, and argues that the author 'does not strive with God, only with himself'. For Brod, Kafka writes out of concern for the contemporary world, and specifically, for the Jews. 'Kafka writes, alongside the general tragedy of mankind, in particular the sufferings of his own unhappy people, homeless, haunted Jewry, the mass without form, without body, as no-one else has ever done. He writes it without the word Jew appearing in any of his books.' Brod sees Kafka as an author of political parables with contemporary resonance, speaking out of a local Jewish experience, i.e. the homelessness of the Jews. He even saw Kafka as a Zionist or potential Zionist who would correct this anomaly through territorial reconcentration of the people in a reconstructed homeland. But Kafka's own words, at least in one specific reaction, belie such a view. After an encounter with Brod and his Zionist notions, he wrote: 'What have I in common with Jews? I have almost nothing in common with myself, and should hide myself quietly in a corner satisfied with the fact that I can breathe' (*Diaries*, entry 8 January 1914). These are not the words of a political activist, let alone of a Zionist sympathiser. It is the expression of someone trying to make sense of himself, achieve inner peace and perhaps harmony with the world too, rather than of one who believes in public or political solutions as a therapy for the human condition. Kafka made an inner voyage through the character of K or his other heroes, where the 'hero' is placed within the confines of a confused world (labyrinth), where judgement was being made and was to be executed in accordance with a mysterious, arbitrary and all but impenetrable law. It is true that the Kafka figure was to fight the situation and the judgement, and inevitably to be defeated by it. The conduct of the struggle, however, does not take place in the political arena within the realms of public polity. The channels of communication are already marked out, and the rules of the game are accepted and adopted. K in *The Trial* has to accept the Advocate granted him, or replace him with another, similar. The Law is still there.

And in the story 'The Judgement' (1912) too, this 'judgement' (here pronounced by the father) has to be accepted. As in *The Trial*, the sentence (for what?) is of death. Brecht pronounced Kafka ultimately a failure as a novelist, because the question of 'whence does guilt proceed?' is never met (Heller). So his work is bound to remain fragmentary. Nothing can arrive as all the staircases are continuously spiral. In 'The Judgement', death is release, and perhaps (only perhaps, because we can not get beyond that point) the solution. The story concludes at the moment of suicide by drowning. 'At this moment an unending stream of traffic was just going over the bridge.' The stream of 'traffic' (in German 'verkehr') is also the word for the sexual intercourse that could grant release. Here is a tale of the absurd which the author himself could not unravel, proceeding from naturalistic narrative by appreciable degrees to its own contradiction. The hero of the story George Bendeman is found writing to a friend away in Russia, informing him of his engagement. But Bendeman has, before sending it off, to show the letter to his father who gets furious, first denying knowledge of the friend and then saying that he knew him so well that he would have had him as a son – a prospect that would have suited the friend excellently. Then the father hurls accusations against his actual son of immorality and of trying to 'cover him up' (choke, kill, replace). It is the father who will not allow the son to marry. And in a deeply irrational but single-mindedly committed moment of hysterical opposition, he condemns the son to his fate.

'The Judgement' is a 'story', but it is similar in plot and tone to the so-called 'Letter to his Father' (1919), an actual letter which was never sent (and was, of course, like so many other of Kafka's writings, only published posthumously). As fiction shades into autobiography with him, so autobiography becomes fiction. Indeed, it was said of Kafka: 'The vicinity of literature and autobiography could hardly be closer than it is with Kafka, indeed it amounts almost to identity. Although in this form it is peculiar to him, it seems at the same time the climax of a chapter in literary history, the history of German writing done by predominantly Jewish writers of Kafka's generation' (Heller). Kafka's undelivered letter hints at many of the author's obsessions. The father is set up as one making a 'judgement' upon the son. He is seen as massive in comparison with the attenuated form of the son, really more a Löwy (the mother's maiden name) in character, mild and sensitive. The father is ambitious, successful, and has above all a 'will to life'. The father then is totally dominant, arbitrary. The metaphor of judgement keeps recurring. The son is a slave operating 'under laws intended for me'. 'Your' (i.e. the boss's) world is remote, inaccessible, unreachable. The two prongs of Kafka's 'activity' are also father dominated – writing and marriage, the former tensely involved with the father and the second as a possibility stunted by him. 'My writing was all about you: all I did there, after all, was to bemoan what I could not bemoan upon your breast. It was an intentionally long drawn out leavetaking from you, only although it was brought about by force on your part, it did take its course in the direction determined by me.' Writing was both his medium of expression and sole source of independence. Marriage however was impossible: 'marrying is barred to me through the fact that it is precisely and peculiarly your most intimate domain.' The father is omnipotent judge — commanding, forbidding, curbing. The son only struggles and writhes pointlessly in his shadow.

No interpretation of Kafka's work can be final, because the strands are not finally tied together. The novel (as usual, unfinished) *America,* as its name suggests, particularly for someone who had never been there, points to newness, excitement, potentiality and discovery. It is the most optimistic of Kafka's stories as foreshadowed in the opening where we read 'a sudden burst of sunshine seemed to illumine the Statue of Liberty'. But the cluster of images is familiar to the Kafka reader. We deal with cases, judgements, justice (of the stoker for example), the labyrinthine path (e.g. round the ship at the end of the voyage), impersonal authority (as that of Uncle Jacob), arbitrary dispensation of verdicts (the uncle's dismissal of Karl) and the search (starting to move around America). There is a mystery. On his dismissal, it is obscure to Karl 'why every minute that keeps me away from my uncle is so important to me'. So in spite of the apparently light tone of the writing, Karl bears the characteristic marks of the Kafka central figure. Let us look at his biography in the novel. He is rejected by his home in Europe, banished by his uncle from his new home, dismissed from employment by the hotel management, misused by his travelling companions, particularly by the domineering Frenchman, Delamarche. He is only accepted by the 'Nature Theatre of Oklahoma' in the final but incomplete chapter. According to Brod's 'postscript', this chapter was to signal reconciliation. But, of course, as we see, the work is incomplete and the reconciliation tentative and potential rather than achieved. Perhaps the 'Nature Theatre' does really stand for that totality of Nature which would absorb everything and everyone, all sinners (those who fail) and Karl himself, another form of the ubiquitous K in the Kafka fiction.

We must ask ourselves though (we cannot help it if we are to survive as readers) what the sense of the judgement is. Who is judging, how, by what and whom? What is maybe the most enduring of the works, the novel *The Trial*, naturally revolves around this. Revolves around without going through to an answer. K is arrested at the beginning of the story, and is executed at the end. We do not know what the charge is and, indeed, K himself ceases to ask what it is soon after his first arrest. The novel was regarded by its author too as unfinished. Others might say that it was doomed to incompleteness as the trial would never reach the highest Court. The story takes place over a year, that is, between first arrest and execution. But K progresses not at all in achievement, comprehension or salvation. He, as perceived from the outside, even by the most unsophisticated observer in the story, is doomed *a priori*. He has the very appearance of a condemned man, and his protests are merely ridiculous. As Franz says about him in the story: 'See Willem, he admits that he doesn't know the Law, and yet he claims he's innocent.' Indeed, he cannot know the Law (as the parable of the delusion indicates), nor the advocates, nor the officials: 'The higher officials keep themselves well hidden.' Justice is out of sight, unfathomable. And as for the Law itself? It is open to interpretation, and there are many commentaries. But however much he might learn, it will be insufficient. The painter, a disreputable character whom K thinks might be of assistance, makes the distinction between what is laid down and the experience itself. In the cathedral where K goes for a putative meeting, he is told a parable by the Priest which is to illustrate the sort of delusion that he is undergoing. This parable is the introduction (writings) that preface the Law itself; it relates of a visitor from the country who seeks entry through the 'door' of the Law. However, the man cannot ever get beyond the first doorkeeper, behind whom there stand many, many more. He persists for years through entreaty, bribery and patience and finally, upon the threshold of death, hears that the 'door' was created solely for him, and is 'now' (i.e. at death) to be closed. Why the patience, why the supplication? What is the point of it all? Who makes the decision? Why was he not informed earlier? All these things are open to interpretation. We may ask however what purpose the door is serving. The man from the country assumed that this was the potential point of access to fulfilment of his ultimate aspiration. But did it not possibly serve to keep the man out rather than to allow him in? Kafka is clearly playing on the climax of the service held on the Day of Atonement, where the prayer is intoned to the Almighty: 'Open a gate for us at a time of the closing of the gate.' The congregation of Israel seeks entry to the divine realm through the repentance of man and the grace of God. In the parable of *The Trial*, each man must needs suffer rejection at the gate created solely for him. The man from the country dies unrewarded and unrequited. K, at the end of the novel, is condemned to death, suffers his punishment willingly, and is despatched. Not honourably, but shamefully. He must die 'like a dog'. The 'process' of the trial (the German word suggests the ongoing movement) is climaxed in the judgement/sentence 'Urteil'). K may not know the outcome *ab initio,* but everyone else including his friends (Fraülein Burstein for example) seems to foresee it. The man from the country arrived with hope and took up his position with patient expectancy. But the doorkeeper had been aware of the necessary denouement all along.

The Castle (also unfinished) represents a moral dominion as well. It is a source of authority but not benevolent authority, not even reasonable authority. However, K patiently pushes on and picks his way through the web, as always unavailingly. We are assured by Brod that the author had intended a positive resolution. 'The ostensible Land Surveyor was to find partial satisfaction at least. He was not to relax in his struggle, but was to die worn out by it. Round his deathbed the villagers were to assemble, and from the Castle itself the word was to come that although K's legal claim to live in the village was not valid, yet, taking certain auxiliary circumstances into account, he was to be permitted to live and work there.' That may be so. But Kafka did conclude the novel thus, and it may be that in view of his repeated assertions of positive intention followed by repeated failure to carry out that intention, he was unable to introduce such a resolution. Even though 'he was to be permitted to live and work there' (an indication of Grace), ultimately his claim was still 'not valid'. The Law, that is the peculiar, ineffable, unapproachable, unknown Law of the world as it is, operates against the land surveyor K. The tone is set by the opening paragraph, where we are informed that 'the Castle hill was hidden' to K. It is not to be significantly exposed to view, understanding or penetration. And as for the man in the story, the struggling, contemptible figure, often a 'K' (without a full name), he can only be reduced, even to a 'gigantic insect' as in 'Metamorphosis' (1912). The status here is the concrete projection of the hero's estimation of himself, and it is absorbed quite naturally within the body of the story. Gregor Samsa of that story seems himself hardly surprised at his changed shape.

For Kafka, in the parable the world is represented by the image of the door by which the man from the country patiently waits in hope of access. But he waits in vain, and the door is closed on him at the point of death. It seems that the prayer of the Jew in the closing service of the Day of Atonement that a door should be opened, is rejected. For another German-Jewish theologian of the period, Franz Rosenzweig (1886-1929), life's work can consist of trying to keep the door open. The movement of his great opus *The Star of Redemption* (1912) is from the reality of death 'into life', which is achieved not by personal immortality, but through the vitality of being Jewish. Rosenzweig wrote this work mainly from the trenches, late in the war, sending the text back home on army postcards. But only a few months previous to the outbreak of war, the author, whose great concern was the revitalisation of Judaism had contemplated conversion to Christianity. He wanted, however, to enter Christianity as a Jew 'through Judaism'. So he went, as he thought, on one last visit, to the synagogue on the Day of Atonement, 1913, and was thus transformed into a Jew. (This is not an experience recorded in his writings, but related by his mother to his biographer Nahum Glatzer.) From this point on, he sought the source of traditional Judaism and its force in contemporary life. He began to see Judaism as being beyond history, metahistorical, fixed in its truth, constantly valid, placed in time but beyond any particular moment. His great teacher, Hegel, had prepounded a system in which History had become God, and was then enclosed in its own laws. For Rosenzweig, God had to stand outside History and thus control it. God's free action involves a threefold process: (1) creation — which establishes the relation between God on the one hand, and, on the other, the world, transitoriness and death; (2) revelation — the point at which God calls out to man; (3) redemption — which frees man from the finality of death through the cycle of the sacred year. Kierkegaard had sought such a development for Christianity, the personal 'leap' of the Christian through faith, beyond fixed law. Rosenzweig saw this transcendence expressed in the past but ongoing experience of the Jewish people. Not through the 'essence of Judaism', as he said in a reference to Leo Baeck, but in response to the constant call 'Hear O Israel'.

Why did Rosenzweig contemplate conversion to Christianity? In one sense, it was simply because he was, as he admitted, living within a Christian context — Christian society, Christian literature, architecture, music, everything, and thus Judaism found itself at an enormous disadvantage. Whereas Christianity could be environmentally just accepted and absorbed naturally, Judaism had to be affirmed against the odds and struggled for through the concrete images of ritual and practice. But Christianity was also viewed (by Christians of course) as the consummation and fulfilment of Judaism. Although a necessary fulfilment. For one with a religious need in twentieth-century Germany, Christianity was a natural cloak.

Then why Judaism after all? Christianity posited the need for Christ. Otherwise, it was impossible to reach the Father. But after this striking period in 1913, Rosenzweig concluded that an intermediary was only necessary for those who were not already with the Father. 'But the situation is quite different for one who does not have to reach the Father because he is already with him. And this is true of the people of Israel (though not of individual Jews). Chosen by its Father, the people of Israel gazes fixedly across the world and history, over to that last, most distant time when the Father, the One and Only, will be "all in all" ' (letter to Rudolf Ehrenberg, 31 October 1913). It was at this point that Rosenzweig pronounced himself in total conformity with Jewish teaching and decided to 'make clear to himself "the entire system of Jewish doctrine" '. And the key to the doctrine is the 'psychological mystery of monotheism. . . As far as I am concerned, God can be whatever he will, but he must be One.' And the notion of revelation must follow from that recognition so that contact with man might be established.

Rosenzweig, from being a peripheral Jew, put Judaism at the centre of his life. And in doing so, he insisted that 'in being Jews we must not renounce anything, but lead everything back to Judaism. From the periphery back to the centre; from the outside, in' (The address at the opening of the Freies Jüdisches Lehrhaus in Frankfurt). Jewish intellectuals from the German-speaking world in the early part of the century had generally, at the most, borne the residual traces of Judaism with pride, but had certainly not regarded Judaism as the fulcrum of their being. So the Buber-Rosenzweig activity indicated a radical reorientation. Rosenzweig thought the main tendencies of contemporary Jewry unsatisfying. Both assimilationists and Zionists were in danger of striving for an attainable goal. And both, if successful in their realisation, would break the link with historical and diaspora Judaism. To be in contact with Judaism was to be in contact with a live, dynamic force, not a closed system. And, as he suggested when still a very young man, the world is the instrument with which the searcher can pierce the abyss. 'Words are tombstones/words are bridges over chasms. One usually walks across without looking down. If one looks down he is liable to feel giddy./ Words are also boards laid over a shaft, concealing it./To be a philosopher is to open tombs, look into abysses, climb down shafts' (*Diary* entry, 17 November 1906). Philosophy (and, of course, theology) is not a safe venture, but a prying open of closed accesses. His function as Jewish theologian was to unsettle the bourgeois complacency of fixed but dead forms in order to resurrect the old but still vital Judaism. A Judaism, by the way, as he discovered during his war postings, that was far from decadent or moribund amongst the confident Sephardi community in Yugoslavia or amongst the masses of Jews in Poland. Here he had a model for peoplehood far beyond the comprehension of those who held it in contempt, the affluent, assimilated and Westernised Germans. Judaism was rather decaying in Germany where it had become crystallised in dead forms.

The other major events of Rosenzweig's life are his founding of the Frankfurt Lehrhaus for the study of Judaism in 1920, and his progressive paralysis which he first noticed not much later, in 1921, shortly after publication of the *Star*. He accepted his lot as part of the necessary whole. Of this fact: 'I myself had only weak and rare intimations. . . but now it is simply true: dying is even more beautiful than living' (letter to Gertrud Opperheim, his lifelong friend, May 1922). And later too, he tried to integrate death unsentimentally. 'Sentimentality is proper for the bystanders. The dying themselves are not sentimental. . . I wouldn't change places with anyone.' His situation did not for one moment interrupt his lifetime devotion to the experience and promotion of Judaism. He characterises the purport of his piece 'The Builders' (an epistle addressed to Buber in 1923 dealing with the place of the Law within Judaism) thus: 'How Christian Jews, rational Jews, religious Jews, Jews from self-defence, sentimentality, loyalty, in short "hyphenated" Jews such as the nineteenth century has produced, can, once again, without danger to themselves or Judaism, become *Jews*' (letter to Eugen Rosenstock, 25 August 1924). He spent his last years working with Buber on a new translation of the Bible, and in presenting the central notions of the *Star* to the general public. This was part of his educational mission that included directing the Lehrhaus or, at the least, taking an active interest in its fortunes, even in his paralysed state. Constantly aware of his terminal condition, he images the way to understanding as barred by a gate which would presumably be unlocked only at the moment of death. But he is getting no nearer this gate: 'When a man stands close to a locked gate he sees no more of what is behind it than if he stands far away from it' (letter to Hans Ehrenburg, 21 June 1925). This image, shared with Kafka, might well have been influenced by Kafka. Certainly Rosenzweig had a tremendous admiration for the novelist, and said that *The Castle* reminded him of the Bible more than did any other book, 'and that is why reading it certainly cannot be called a pleasure'.

Rosenzweig's thought is existential, that is it takes its starting point from the thinking person himself. 'I believe that a philosophy, to be adequate, must rise out of the thinking that is done from the personal standpoint of the thinker. To achieve being objective, the thinker must proceed boldly from his own subjective situation' (*The Star of Redemption*). And 'all knowledge of the whole has its source in death, in the fear of death' (ibid). Throughout this great work, he relentlessly opposed the dualism of body/soul, the closed circle of history as drawn by Hegel, and any pretended effort to formulate thought by stepping out of the experience of the striving subject. Whereas philosophy would nullify death by non-recognition of it as meaningful, his 'new thinking' would proceed from it. Death is the recognition of life. It is not a machine outside the body that writes philosophy. The challenge of this new thinking (from Schopenhauer and through Nietzsche) was that it replaced the conception of the world (Weltanschauung) with a conception of life (Lebensanschauung). Traditional philosophy 'has always inquired into the essence of things' ('The New Thinking', 1925). But 'what the new philosophy, the new thinking, actually does is to employ the method of sound common sense as a method of scientific thinking'. The thought is bound to its time and situation. 'At every moment, cognition is bound to that very moment and cannot make its past not passed, or its future not coming.' Revelation is also central to the scheme, because although God must be separate (otherwise man would be worshipping himself), yet he must also be knowable. The new thinking is concerned with language, its dynamic, modification and changes, with human relationships and the way that these are modified, and with God too, but in the way that one enters into a live relationship with Him. God then is not an abstract category, posited by logic. For that, revelation would be superfluous and therefore impossible. Also, He would be assessible to those of highest and most dedicated intellect, and only to those. Not to every live human being. The 'new theory of knowledge' demands that contact with God be realised in active life. It is not interested in generally agreed truth, mathematical truth, tautological truth, but rather in those matters for which man is willing to pay, even with his life. The new thinking opposes isms with what looks like another ism but is not — 'absolute empiricism'.

We must invoke too, as springing from this belief characterisation of Jewish thought in the area, Rosenzweig's collaborator and older colleague, Martin Buber (1878-1965), better known to the general public than Rosenzweig himself. He was in one a reviver of Judaism, proponent of humanistic Zionism, rediscoverer of Hasidism, interpreter of the Biblical word and propounder of meaningful dialogue, between man and man and between man and God. Buber's *I and Thou* (1922) in characterised by Rosenzweig as being part of the new thinking. This work is central to Buber's theoretical concerns on all social, religious and Jewish matters. Like Rosenzweig he seeks a starting point for procedure. Like him, he takes the individual experiencing life as the primary situation. For Buber though, the primary experience is relationship. And it is this relationship which is of two sorts. I-Thou and I-It. The I does not exist in itself, but is dependent on the character of its relating. And as for the second category: 'The I of the primary word I-It, that is, the I faced by no Thou but surrounded by a multitude of contents, has no present, only the past.' So I-It has contained the It, categorised it. 'It' becomes a 'was'. On the other hand, 'Thou has no bounds'. 'Thou' has not been bounded, 'thou' lives on — a vital, continuing, self-modifying experience to the 'I'.

Buber has been much discussed and analysed (e.g. in Diamond), and his written work is so readily available as to make any further and necessarily cursory characterisation otiose. But he is also rightly in place, not just as a spokesman for that German Jewry, but as a current voice too. German Jewry was manifold in its ambition, scope and intellectual achievement. It also represents the first attempt in the modern world to set up a total, uncompromising Judaism, that does not, on the one hand, retreat from the modern world (including its thought), nor, on the other, reduce itself in order to try to adjust to that world. It absorbs it rather than is absorbed by it. No-one has etched its atmosphere and obscure challenges more chillingly than Kafka in a series of pregnant images. But others have also attempted to come to terms with it through re-interpretation, study and re-viewing both the traditional sources and present-day experience. Alas, the consummation was short-lived and perhaps, thereby falsified. Jewish life in Germany (and the German-speaking world) went through assimilation, orthodoxy, cultural symbiosis and revivalism. But after the Great War, it lasted scarcely a generation. Its fate after 1933 is a pathetic tailpiece to a fascinating story.

4 IN THE EYE OF THE REVOLUTION: RUSSIA

Russian Jewry (in the broad sense of Jewry within the great Russian Empire) had become the largest in the world during the course of the nineteenth century. According to the 1887 census, the Jewish population was then about five-and-a-half million, having risen from only about one million at the beginning of the century (Sachar). The major factors in this dramatic rise were the incorporation by Russia of former 'Congress' Poland, together with other territories, and natural increase, greater proportionally than the natural increase and survival of other sections of the population. This took place only in a small part of the Russian territories, an area of about 362,000 square miles, i.e. about 20 per cent of European Russia – in Lithuania, Latvia, Poland, Byelorussia and the Ukraine. Jewry had been absorbed reluctantly under Czarist rule and confined to these areas, known as the 'Pale of Settlement', areas where Jews were permitted to reside (although this permission too underwent changes and modification).

The great period of Russian liberalism came to an end with the assassination of the reformist Czar Alexander II in 1881. Literature and thought had flourished to an unprecedented degree. The last 30 years had given the world so many of the permanent Russian classics, a radical restatement of the implications of the Western Enlightenment, an absorption and transformation of Western thought, and a fundamentally new contribution to literature (particularly the novel) across a very broad spectrum of experiment and achievement. The indirect implications of this were Russian Jewry's self-enlightenment and its partial willingness to go along with the process of Russification. The ambivalence of the host environment could be seen in a historical context as a phase passing into a new era of mutual acceptance and growing identity of outlook and behaviour. But the increasing population, poverty, industrial and social ferment also proceeded apace. The Jews were not accepted on the whole by the nobility, by the peasants, or even (as we shall see) by the intelligentsia. The assassination of the Czar sparked off a wave of pogroms such as had never hitherto been witnessed – systematic, widespread, officially approved. The Jewish leadership and masses were shocked and many reappraised their position. This period marked the burgeonings of a proto-Zionism ('Hibat Zion'), an ethnic Socialism (the Bund), and a massive wave of emigration which went on for three or four decades. Locally, conditions became tougher. The so-called 'May laws' were introduced (3 May 1882), whereby Jews were not allowed to resettle in rural areas, even in the Pale, and restrictions on entry into the professions and universities were raised massively. By the end of the century 40 per cent of Jewry was dependent on charity. (And these 'May laws' were to remain in force until March 1917.)

Ideologically, Jewry divided itself into: (1) those who wanted out, either in the short or long term, and therefore sought a more secure existence through emigration; (2) those who turned more and more to a specific form of Jewish nationalism, to what was later to be called Zionism; (3) those who began to seek a partial Jewish solution within the existing bodies through social change and the new Socialism; (4) those who pinned their hopes on a national or even worldwide revolution which would project an end to the Jewish problem. No Jew could reasonably favour Czarism, which was explicitly and exclusively Christian, and which became increasingly anti-Jewish. So the Jewry that remained in Russia until and beyond 1917 was largely reformist or revolutionary. Not necessarily Bolshevik of course. Bolshevism was, after all, only one branch (and not in 1917 the 'majority' one) of just one of the revolutionary groupings, the SDs (Social Democrats). But in the early stages of the revolutionary period, they were at least not anti-revolutionary, and in the civil war, they suffered enormous ravages under the Whites. After the Great War (Poland, of course, was not split off) anti-Jewish measures were again introduced. For example, as early as 1918 the Bund was declared illegal (Gilbert).

The concern in this chapter is with the post-revolutionary phase, although set in the context of the Russian tradition. It is two-pronged – with the literature by Jews and the literature about Jews (usually both), as an expression of the Soviet Union. It is a fairly new product anyway. 'Literature in Russia, in the modern sense of the word, is a fairly recent phenomenon, dating back not more than 200 years, while Jewish participation in it, however modest, begins only in mid 19th century' (Friedberg a). Jews had simply not been Russian writers until late in the nineteenth century, and thus entry then took on a problematic character. The social reality of Slavism was not only non-Jewish but hostile to Jews, militantly Christian, ethnic, xenophobic, with a specifically anti-Jewish tendency manifest too even amongst the greatest Russian writers. The Jew appears rarely in nineteenth-century Russian literature, and then usually as caricature

(Friedberg b). And in Soviet literature, Jews are accepted in so far as they renounce their own ethnic links and associate themselves with Sovietism. The hero of I. Ehrenburg's novel *Stormy Life of Lazik Roitschwartz* (1927), for example, the Jewish tailor Lazik and son of a Rabbi becomes a Communist commissar. The official disapproval of any Jewish ethnicity expressed in literature, history, folklore, or even memorials, was to become further pronounced with the passing of years, in the post-Stalin era as well. Ehrenburg has recalled in his *Memoirs* that he could not publish a book about the Nazi slaughter of Soviet Jews, although he and others were encouraged to publicise Nazi atrocities in general. We will see later how the Jewish situation has persisted in retaining a problematic character in Soviet letters. This is so just because of the determination with which it is denied and eradicated even when the context demands its presence.

We can see this in Ehrenburg's published work too. Although it is difficult with him as with all officially published (and therefore officially approved) work to disentangle his own voluntary contribution from the imposed line.

Russian literary anti-Semitism goes back to the origins of the literature itself. Nikolay Gogol, writing in the 1830s and 1840s, typically represents the Jews as primitive, untrustworthy, treacherous, superstitious and solely concerned with money. The Jew of his novella *Taras Bulba* is a caricature universal in time and place. Yankel is a 'revenue farmer and tavernkeeper' and (from noblemen and gentlemen) 'had slowly sucked most of their money and had strongly impressed his presence on that locality. For a distance of three miles in all directions not a single farm remained in a proper state.' We see him too in his religious practice 'turning to spit for the last time, according to the forms of his creed'. As for money: 'he tried to stifle within him the eternal thought of gold which twines like a snake about the soul of a Jew'. This is contradistinction to the noble Cossack, one such as Taras who lives only to fight and kill for his honour, his Ukrainian homeland and his orthodox Christianity. In the Russian literary tradition, the Cossack can be the repository of all the simple virtues. After all, simplicity is a virtue much admired in theory by the complex intellectual. We see this view here with Gogol, in Tolstoy's *The Cossacks*, written two or three decades later, and then again, paradoxically, in those masterful stories by the Jewish Soviet writer, Isaac Babel, in his first published collection of stories *Red Cavalry* (1929). The first-person narrator there, bespectacled, intellectual, residually Jewish, aspired to natural acceptance on the part of the totally physical Cossacks. This is integral to the situation. The Jewish writer in the Soviet Union sees himself through the eyes of the Russian and Soviet intelligentsia, and so for the most part makes a fundamentally negative assessment of his Jewishness on the basis of a negative perception. This is expressed in different ways by the three writers who constitute the principal subject to this chapter – Babel, Mandelstam and Pasternak. Babel associates with the Cossack enemy. Mandelstam (the thinker) has a memory of Jewish chaos, and Pasternak's characters talk about transcending Judaism.

Nadezhda Mandelstam (1899-1980) was scarcely known at all, even to the Soviet public, before the publication in the West of the two volumes, *Hope against Hope* (1970) and *Hope Abandoned* (1973), describing her own and her husband's (Osip's) life and work, and the larger context of the Soviet intelligentsia. To such a degree had Osip Mandelstam (1891-1938) kept his own detailed biography out of his publications that his readers were not even certain that he had been married (Mandelstam, *Prose*). But then Nadezhda produced this major opus which won great acclaim, and which in itself is a remarkable literary and spiritual testimony. It communicates not only of her devotion and self-sacrifice in the cause of her husband's work but also her own achievement in building up a picture of life and literature in the face of totalitarian repression. Totalitarianism is a word often used lightly. But the Soviet system, particularly from 1934 onwards, represented the apotheosis of arbitrary terror and control. Mandelstam (here referred to as M) was first arrested in 1934 (Eugenia Ginzburg also indicates that the Terror of 1936/7 really opened in 1934), a period during which people still were accustomed to asking why. Many, even later, when practically everyone of consequence was being arrested and sentenced to exile, torture and execution, pondered the reason for their treatment. Nadezhda in *Hope against Hope*, quotes the poetess Akhmatova about arrests: 'What do you mean, what for? It's time you understood that people are arrested for nothing.' It is true that M had written a very derogatory poem about Stalin which he had read out to a group of people (possibly at Pasternak's home), and that he had been reported. But M had already been in disfavour since 1923 when his name was crossed off a list of people permitted to write for official publications. The title of Nadezhda's two volumes, a pun on her own name meaning 'hope' indicate the progressive recognition that nothing can be done publicly to withstand the tightening grip of the total terror. The maximal achievement is the preservation of one's own humanity. M's career means just that. His writing was always a private statement rejecting the accepted wisdom and the political yoke. In 1930, Stalin wrote a letter in *Bolshevik* which stated that nothing should be published that was at variance with the official point of view! This cemented his control, and petrified potential initiative.

These memoirs help us to understand the background to the situation and the complicity of the intelligentsia in its creation. Nadezhda quotes Herzen who said that the intelligentsia so much feared its own people that it was willing to be in chains itself provided that the people too remained fettered. There was a dread of chaos and longing for order. Her brother ascribed the decisive factor in this complicity to the word 'revolution' a word which no intellectual could bear to surrender. 'It is a word to which whole nations have succumbed, and its force was such that one wonders why our rulers still needed prisons and capital punishment.' M was different, isolated, not subservient to transient fashions, not attracted to creeds, not even swayed by history. Pasternak, for example, she says, was a more official figure; M was a nomad. Of course, there is no implication that Pasternak toed the prevalent line, or was a public spokesman. It presumably means that Pasternak was concerned with the public domain, and aspired to record history and development. We will see in *Doctor Zhivago* that the characters, particularly the central ones, are witnesses to great events. Mandelstam recorded a private world. It was one that naturally impinged on the public sphere too, but this private world, increasingly compounded, complex and difficult, was not historically delimited. For him, history was in the wings, and was, in the long run, virtually irrelevant.

Sometimes though, the physical pressure of the immediate present is too demanding. Even M was prepared in 1936 to write an ode to Stalin in order to try and save his wife and, thus, his poetry (we should note that if it were not for Nadezhda's efforts, M's poetry would have not survived). She writes: 'whenever at some point on earth, mortal terror and the pressure of utterly insoluble problems are present in a particularly intense form, general questions about the nature of being receded into the background. How could we stand in awe before the forces of nature and the eternal laws of existence if terror of a mundane kind was felt so tangibly in everyday life?' Nadezhda lives very much in the public sphere. Life in the 1930s had changed and changed people with it. Even the nature of happiness had changed: 'We have lost the capacity to be spontaneously cheerful and it will never come back to us.' Although public misery had to be renounced too, because discontent could imply counter-revolutionism. Like Ginzburg, Nadezhda points out that women survive better in the long run. 'The men seemed stronger and withstood the first shocks, but then their hearts gave out and very few lived to be seventy.' The Terror had succeeded in its object of general intimidation: 'To plunge the whole country into a chronic fear the numbers of victims must be raised to astronomical levels.' M had no connection with this public sphere, although interestingly enough in contrast, Babel knew Yezhov, the head of the NKVD personally, and associated with the Chekists. Why? To touch death with his fingers? 'No,' Babel replied. 'I don't want to touch it with my fingers — I just like to have a sniff and see what it smells like.'

In this atmosphere, prose, poetry and its readers became a special thing — the people involved were a breed apart. M said: 'The keepers of the flame hid in dark corners, but the flame did not go out. It is there for all to see. It is there for all to see.' But there was no resistance because everyone was crushed, the killers as much as their victims, trapped by a system which they had helped to build. Nadezhda was a fighter as much as anyone, supporting her husband, accompanying him, recording his poetry and preserving it, struggling as much as possible to free him, and then seeking his rehabilitation. M died in uncertain circumstances, officially on 27 December 1938. But there was no proof of death, and in any case 'a person could be considered dead from the moment he was sent to a camp, or indeed, from the moment of his arrest which was automatically followed by his conviction and sentence to imprisonment in a camp.'

Hope Abandoned, Nadezhda's later and longer volume, aspires to a broader view of the situation beyond specific biography. She notes the prevalence of Jews amongst the new intelligentsia. 'Where have so many Jews come from, after all the pogroms and the gas chambers. . . The fact is that the resurgent intelligentsia of the present consists of Jews and half Jews — though they often come from grimly positivist families in which the parents go on mounting the same old ossified balderdash. Many of the younger one have also become Christians, or think on religious lines.' She desires a revulsion from tyranny, positivism and materialism. And she too can now define herself as a Jew in her ability to keep on against the odds, even with 'hope abandoned'. She belongs 'to a mysterious tribe which persist despite all the laws of history and logic'. She is a member of this living, suffering group, each suffering doubly — the lot of his own people and also 'the misfortune of those in whose country they have put up their tents'. Her books are a record of such persistent, successful survival in adversity.

But the life to which she dedicated herself was that of her husband Osip, as poet and human being who surived in the work that she preserved. He started his writing career before the Great War, and published a book of poems, *Stone*, in 1913. His early poetry was written in the manner of the Symbolists, and dealt with poetry itself and architecture. His second collection *Tristia* appeared in 1922, and in 1928, the summit period of his career and reputation, he produced a collected edition of his poetry and a volume of prose. In the 1930s his troubles began in earnest, and official approval was removed. Then he was arrested, attempted suicide. After being released he was again arrested, and died in the camps.

Mandelstam's prose is poetic. Rather than develop a consecutive narrative, it creates atmosphere by association of images. Sometimes, it is difficult to follow the thread which is consequential through the sequence of objects, words and notions rather than through plot. In 'The Noise of Time' (1925), his first story, he presents a picture of a life that is dying — literal decadence. The scene described in the disappearing world of Judaism that has clung to the author like an ancient burr. This world is often contrasted to the more attractive and Gentile life around. 'All the elegant mirage of Petersburg was merely a dream, a brilliant covering thrown over the abyss, while round about there sprawled the chaos of Judaism — not a motherland, not a hearth, but precisely a chaos, the unknown womb whence I had issued, which I feared, about which I made vague conjectures and fled always fled ... the strange, cheerless holidays, grating upon the ear with their harsh names: Rosh Hashana and Yom Kippur.' This negative perception of the phenomenon does not infringe the recognition that it remains his source. And the source is so powerful that it permeates everything around, however seemingly nugatory. 'As a little bit of mush fills an entire house, so the last influence of Judaism overflows all of one's life. O, what a strong smell that is! Could I possibly not have noticed that in real Jewish houses there was a different smell from that in Aryan houses?' And as for the books there, so precious to him, permanent companions in life, they are arranged on the bookshelf in order of priority corresponding to the arrangement of world literature itself. The Jewish shelf was lowest, 'chaotic ... This was the Judaic chaos thrown into the dust. This was the level to which any Hebrew primer, which I never master, quickly fell.' And then the German shelf. 'All this was my father fighting his way as an autodidact back into the German world out of the Talmudic wilds.' The poet never heard

Yiddish in his childhood, and finds everything in the synagogue unrefined and vulgar. His 'acmeism' is a counterpart to that background and in his view connects him to the best of Europe. The purpose of this prose piece is 'to speak not about myself but to track down the age, the noise and the germination of time'. He reaches out here to a historical sense and ambition in order to encapsulate the period, to see it as a unity, although a unity gone 'shattered, finished, unrepeatable'.

A later story, 'The Egyptian Stamp' (1928), is seen mainly through the eyes of one of the characters rejoicing in the strange name of Parnok, imaged as sheep and bird. He trips with 'his little sheep hooves', and speaks to women 'in a wild, bombastic language, and exclusively about the loftiest matters'. The author's images are transferred by association to a different frame, e.g. on a visit to the dentist: 'And Parnok spun like a top down the gap-toothed intended stair, leaving the dumbfounded dentist before the sleeping cobra of his drill.' The image conjures up the subject. But who is speaking? Because suddenly a first-person narrator intervenes, who begs to be distinguished from the leading protagonist. 'Lord! Do not make me like Parnok! Give me the strength to distinguish myself from him. For I also have stood in that terrifying, patient line which creeps towards the yellow window of the box office.' The danger that the narrator might be his chief protagonist Parnok is confirmed later, but then with relief: 'What a pleasure for the narrator to switch from the third person to the first.' As he abhorred the chaos of Judaism in 'The Noise of Time' so now he notes its sadness: 'In Jewish apartments there reigns a menancholy, bewhiskered silence.' And what really terrifies our implied narrator is the possibility of arbitrary meaninglessness: 'It is terrifying to think that our life is a tale without a plot, or hero, made up of desolation and glass, out of the feverish babble of constant digressions, out of the delirium of the Petersburg influenza!' And what about history? Surely the great events of 1917 must be recorded. He remarks of that that we now write 'railroad prose'. And he enjoins himself: 'Destroy your manuscript, but save whatever you have inscribed in the margin out of boredom, out of helplessness, and as it were, in a dream.' He values not the consecutive, standardised, official, planned account, but the subliminal and surreal that emerge from the back of the mind and that unconsciously control the pen.

The poetry asserts the uniquely individual and so quintessentially human. He cannot and does not ignore the impingement of the ugly system. As in 'The Apartment'

'It won't be the fountain Hippocrene
that will burst through the back-work walls,
but the current of household terror
in this evil coop in Moscow'
                    (1933)

He images a total transformation of the public world in 'The Age'.

'My animal, my age, who will ever be able to look into your eyes?
Who will ever glue back together the vertebrae
of two centuries with his blood?'
                    (1923, revised 1936)

The change that has taken place is indeed so dramatic that the human
being has no more to say. He is cast solid in a mould. In 'He who Finds
a Horseshoe'

'Human lips
that have no more to say
keep the shape of the last word they said,
and the hand goes on feeling the full weight
even after the jug
has splashed itself half empty
on the way home
— What I'm saying now isn't said by me.
It's dug out of the ground like grains of petrified wheat.'

The onset of dumbness that Mandelstam is said to have professed recalls
Babel's reference in his speech at the Writers' Congress of 1934 to his
mastery of the new 'genre of silence'. He praises the life that exists, as
long as it is lived with dignity:

'Opulent poverty, regal indigence!
Live in it calmly, be at peace. Blessed are these days, these nights,
and innocent is the labour's singing sweetness.'

Important is the feel of the solid earth beneath the feet, and the times that
are out of joint no longer possess that luxury. This is the crux and opening of the Stalin poem/epigram: 'Our lives no longer feel ground under

them.' Stalin is also imaged in terms of animals, but, in his case, of repulsive animals. He has 'worms' for fingers, 'cockroaches' on his upper lip. He is 'ringed with a scum of chicken-necked bosses' who, for their part, cannot produce human speech: 'One whistles, another meouws, a third snivels.' Only Stalin himself can produce a majestic sound. Not speech, of course, but a boom.

He has poems of despair too. In 'Moscow 1933', he compares himself to a stream with

> two faces, one forward,
> one backward, and one is sweet and hard'.

He is divided, looking in both directions. But now there is no relief:

> 'and one way the old sighing frees me no longer,
> and the other way the goal can no longer be seen!'

He can no longer derive comfort from either the solidity of the past or the expectation of the future. His creed is humanist in sum; man needs the earth, needs his country, his language, his books, his cities. But it is only man that is significant, and these other things exist for the sake of man:

> 'Let the names of imperial cities
> caress the ears with brief meaning.
> It's not Rome the city that lives on,
> it's man's place in the universe.'

Mandelstam tried to live a genuinely human life, and to write authentically human poetry within a dehumanising environment.

The career of Isaac Babel (1894-1941) like that of so many other Soviet writers was ambivalent. Originating in Odessa, about which so many of his stories revolve, he settled in St Petersburg in 1915. He later fought for the Reds in the civil war in Eastern Poland together with the Cossack cavalry, an experience which forms the bedrock of experience for his first collection of published stories *Red Cavalry*. He published *Tales of Odessa* in 1932, after the dissolution of RAPP, the Association demanding proletarian consciousness in literature. He also wrote two plays and some other stories. He recognised that his output was very limited, and, at the 1934 Congress, he talked about practising silence. Arrested in 1939, he was never heard from again. Publicly, he appeared sympathetic to the regime, or at least acquiescent to it, and he protested loyalty. But, like all the others, he was concerned with survival. The irony of his perception comes over more by implication than in direct statement.

His view of the Jew is also bifurcated. There is the Jew of Odessa and the Jew of Poland. The first is typified by the gangster Benya Kirk, tough guy of the Moldavanka, and the latter, cringing, helpless, bearded, bespectacled. But who is the narrator himself? Babel too is bespectacled, scholarly and, in his view, distorted. In 'Awakening', he writes auto-biographically and confesses: 'How slow was my acquisition of the things one needs to know! In my childhood, chained to the Gemara, I had led the life of a sage. When I grew up I started climbing trees.' The normal, 'healthy' progress of a child to adulthood is reversed for him, as for the archetypal Jew that he meets again in Poland. In this story he has described himself explicitly. But the narrator emerges implicitly through the pared-down descriptions of the battleground. His principal ambition is to be accepted by his companions, and so reject his inherited nature and overt characteristics. He does not want to inhabit the frame of the bespectacled, intellectual Jew with which he is saddled. He aspires to the ruthless physicality of the Cossack soldier. So he distances himself from the Jews that he meets, and speaks of them as though they are odd, not connected with him at all, as an exotic breed foreign to him. When he is billeted with Jews, he writes: 'In the room I was given I discovered turned-out wardrobes, scraps of women's fur coats on the floor, human filth, fragments of the occult crockery the Jews use only once a year, at Easter time.' He then extols the virtues of mercilessness, and exclaims: 'everywhere was treachery and full of dirty Yids like under the old regime' ('Crossing into Poland'). These are not the observations of a Jew, even of a secularised Jew. They are rather the hostile marks of an outsider, implacably superior. Is this the author's guise as narrator? He does, after all, aspire to the position of Cossack, so why should he not adopt the perspective and language of the Cossack warrior?

But he can adopt another guise too, even in the same series of stories, their action taking place in the same environment. He can be a Jew with Gedali. In the story 'Gedali', he conjures up a memory of Jewish melancholy childhood in the terms of a sentimental dirge. Those Sabbath eves: 'On those evenings my child's heart was rocked like a little ship upon enchanted waves. O the rotted Talmuds of my childhood! O the dense melancholy of memories!' Quite a different narrator! And the refraction of his sympathy is so different. Because now we hear the reaction of the orthodox Jew to the revolution. And Gedali is prepared to accept this revolution. But he wants to preserve his own tradition as well. 'The Revolution — we will say "yes" to it, but are we to say "no" to the Sabbath?' It is not that Gedali will not accept the revolution, but that the revolution does not seem to want to accept Gedali. It only shoots. In fact, both the revolution and the counter-revolution shoot. How is one to tell which is which? That old world, as Mendalstam also indicated in his prose and poetry, is dead. Gedali 'mourns'. 'Gedali,' I said, 'today is Friday and it's already evening. Where are Jewish biscuits to be got, and a Jewish glass of tea, and a little of that pensioned-off God in a glass tea?' These are simply not to be had; Jewish biscuits, Jewish tea and the Jewish God are no longer in evidence. The narrator does not comment on this, just as he does not obtrude his conclusions when he adopts a different tone in other stories.

Babel makes the contrast between the old types of Jew explicit. In his encounter with the Jews of Poland, he recalls his own experience in the Ukraine: 'The image of the stout and jovial Jews of the South, bubbling like cheap wine, took shape in my memory, in sharp contrast to the bitter scorn inherent in these long bony backs, these tragic yellow beards. In these passionate, anguish-chiselled features, there was no fat, no warm pulsing of blood.' Again, it is not clear from this statement what the status of the narrator is in the matter, whether he identifies himself with the group that he observes. Because he then accepts the stereotype of the Jew as entrepreneur and exploiter whom the Reds must suppress: 'The Jews have tied with threads of gain the Russian peasant to the Polish Pen, the Czech colonist to the factory in Lodz. They were smugglers, the ablest on the frontier and nearly always staunch defenders of their faith. Hasidism kept that superstitious population of hawkers, brokers and tavern-keepers in stifling captivity' ('Berestechko'). No word here of Jewish disabilities, restriction on movement, opportunity, residence and trade. The observation is totally negative, as made by an enemy. Again it is the Red warrior speaking out of the experience of a Cossack, Christian tradition. The narrator (ironically?) seeks a convincing disguise. 'Bent beneath the funeral garland, I continued on my way, imploring fate to grant me the simplest of proficiences — the ability to kill my fellow men' (conclusion of 'After the Battle'). Finally, he recounts the fulfilment of his ambition after straining for this acceptance: 'Months passed and my dreams came true. The Cossacks stopped watching me and my horse'

('Argamak'). They took him for granted, and accepted him unquestioningly. He had proved that he could kill, fight and ride.

The Tales of Odessa are so different in tone that you could think that they had been written by someone else. The author reflects on his childhood and recreates it, not naturalistically, but in full-blooded enjoyment of the grotesque and the ridiculous. These stories were written in the 1920s although published later, and contrast with *Red Cavalry* in every way. Benya Krik is the archetypal contrast to the passive yellow beard, or to Gedali. He is competent, full-blooded, in control, unscrupulous, physical. The tone is facetious. He talks about 'killing live people'. Lyubka the Cossack (in a story of that name) is the nickname given to Mrs Lyubka Shneiveis, a landlady and brothel keeper. The author recounts the exploits of Benya Krik, known as 'the king', how he married the daughter of the 'one-eyed Rook', and so greatly increased his wealth and control. And Babel's other stories too are witty, mixing the memorial with the aspirant. One of the fascinating things about Babel as a writer is how he manages to combine the self-revelatory form, the autobiographical mode (first or third person) with a gnomic impersonality and ambivalence. But his stories are regarded universally as the most masterful produced in the Soviet phase of Russian literature.

In many respects, Boris Pasternak (1890-1960) resembles Osip Mandelstam. They regarded themselves as very different types of poets. (See the report of the famous conversation between Stalin and Pasternak about Mandelstam. Stalin asked for Pasternak's opinion about the other after Mandelstam had come to unwelcome attention. Pasternak noted the difference in poetic character between them, although he confirmed Mandelstam's quality.) But they both had a background of Symbolism, both put a great deal of stress on the use of image, both asserted individual values in the face of State pressure, both came in for official disapproval by the Authorities from the late 1930s onward, and both were of Jewish background, rejecting that background in various ways. Pasternak was the more prolific writer, principally a poet. But here, I am going to restrict my consideration to the large scale novel that he produced, *Doctor Zhivago,* which was never published in Russia. It became indeed a major link and source of information about the events in the Soviet Union for the Western world. Particularly was it a source of information about the revolutionary period and the local intellectual's reaction to it. Unlike Mandelstam, Pasternak aspired to grasp history and the specific nature of great events in Russia. The book, for all that it is more poetic than novelistic, is permeated with a sense of historic significance with which the protagonists attempt to come to terms. *Doctor Zhivago* is fairly weak in narrative writer's virtues. The characters are often mouthpieces for views rather than live figures, and the development is imposed rather than emerging from plot and character. But it is strong in recall of mood, in its use of image, in its presentation of idea and conflict, and in the general sense of drama. Indeed, a work which takes as its subject the build-up to the revolution, the year 1905, the revolution itself, the civil war, and a passionate but illicit love affair conducted against this backdrop, could hardly fail to grip the reader.

The novel tells the story of Zhivago from his early childhood until his premature death. He trains as a doctor so that he can be independent and useful, but his inclination is towards a preoccupation with poetry, some of which is presented at the end of the novel. The book is a picture of the period as seen by Zhivago, his family, his friends and his beloved Lara. Two things emerge. One is the significance of the present era. The second is that truth can only be grasped by the individual. Zhivago's Uncle Kolya, the influential intellectual, voices this view which is reinforced even more strongly by Zhivago himself: 'It is always a sign of mediocrity in people when they herd together, whether their group loyalty is to Solovyev or to Kant or Marx. The truth is sought only by individuals, and they break with those who do not love it enough.'

But a subliminal preoccupation of the novel is what it means to be Jewish. Not that this is seen as a very positive thing. The author's view is not stated, nor is the chief protagonist's. Zhivago acts as a sounding board for the views of others. He observes, listens and records these and the overall state of things. He has a close friend, Misha Gordon (Gordon is a common Jewish name in Russia), who speculates on the Jewish question even at the age of eleven. 'What did it mean to be a Jew? What was the purpose of it? What was the reward or the justification of this unarmed challenge which brought nothing but grief?' That to be Jewish means to suffer is accepted as axiomatic by all observers. Zhivago himself comments on the position of the Jews during the terrible events of the civil war to Lara. 'You can't imagine what this wretched Jewish population is going through in this war. The fighting happens to be in their Pale of Settlement. And as if punitive taxation, the destruction of their property and all their other suffering were not enough, they had to put up with pogroms, insults and the charge that they lack patriotism.' In fact, the view of Zhivago, the non-Jew, are more sympathetic to the Jews than of the Jew Gordon. Not that he justifies this persistent Jewish existence. But he does sympathise with the double portion of suffering, a feature noted too by Nadezhda Mandelstam in *Hope Abandoned*. The Jew suffers both as part of the general condition, and for the added factor of being Jewish. What seems to puzzle the protagonists though is why the Jews need to exist as a nation, if indeed they do voluntarily. Gordon is moving into a Christian phase, and he holds that the Gospels preach beyond nations to individuals. 'Why don't they (i.e. the leaders) say to them (i.e. the Jewish fold) "that's enough, stop now. Don't hold on to your identity, don't all act together in a crowd. Disperse. Be with all the rest. You are the first and best Christians in the world." ' Christianity has superceded Judaism, and the Jew who has himself gone through the process of conversion and evolution, in a historical sense, is uniquely well placed to be Christian. As it was he who brought Christianity into being, he can be a more authentic Christian than any non-Jew.

Later in the novel, Lara echoes these views and adds a utilitarian rider. ' "It's so strange that these people who once brought about the liberation of mankind from the yoke of idolatry, and so many of whom now devote themselves to its liberation from unjustice, should be powerless to achieve their own liberation from themselves, from the yoke of their loyalty to an obsolete, antediluvian designation which has lost all meaning — that they should not rise above themselves and dissolve among all the rest, whose religion they have founded and with whom they would have so much in common if they knew them better." ' The paradox in this view is that the Jews have extended liberation to others in the past (through Christianity) and continue to do so in the present (though their revolutionary struggle for general freedom). But they have neither managed to achieve their own physical liberation (they continue to undergo persecution) nor spiritual liberation by transcending a primitive and now outdated form of religious practice and ethnic identification.

Contemporary history is the focus of the book, and the individual observes it. At first, he enthuses about his privilege. Zhivago says: ' "Do you realise what an unheard of thing is happening? Such a thing happens once in an eternity. Just think of it, the whole of Russia has had its roof torn off, and you and I and everyone else are out in the open." ' And on reflection: 'He understood that he was a pygmy before the monstrous machine of the future.' He just stands in awe of the events and admires those in control who dare take History by the neck to strangle it or give it new direction. But then later, doubts creep in.

After all, horrors are on the increase, not diminishing. Whatever was worthwhile in the old is not being perserved, and the status of the new is uncertain and faltering. The individual virtues are the sole resilient ones. The remarkable feature of life is love, such a love as that between him and Lara. Others may well indeed experience such love, without perceiving it as something remarkable. Grand notions of History have led people astray. Only love is harmonious; war is terrible and the cause of falsehood. This realisation allows Zhivago to write poetry once more, although he feels that the main part of the work was being done not by him but by something above him and controlling him. He only allowed the contact and recorded the message. (Mandelstam also expressed the feeling that it was not he who truly wrote his poetry, but something else that took over and inhabited his body and senses.)

The novel reports a conversation conducted long after Zhivago's death, in the form of an epilogue, when Gordon reflects on what has happened. Now, after all, the thing can be seen whole. The Revolution, however noble and splendid it seemed, became coarsened. It happens in history that things loftily conceived degenerate in practice over the course of time. Rome derived from Greece, and the Russian Revolution emerged from the Russian Enlightenment. And the reader might observe that one should not be so easily taken in either by a passing fashion or by public and general acclamation. Perhaps there are underlying values more worthwhile than those embodied in such a dramatic canvas with its immediate attraction.

Any consideration of high quality Soviet literature must inevitably revolve around dissident writers and material smuggled out and published in the West. One can never be certain of the authenticity of the local product, to what degree actual or potential censorship has been exercised. So a whole literature has become problematic, and the availability of texts is haphazard. Ilya Ehrenburg (1891-1967) has managed to straddle the divergent paths of foreign residence, Jewishness and official approval. He even died a natural death. A prolific author, foreign correspondent and novelist, he dared to attack the Bolsheviks in the early days of the regime (Hingley), and went abroad until 1924. He spent many further periods abroad. He had been in France, he reported the civil war in Spain, World War II (what the Soviets call the Great Patriotic War) in Germany. Then he went to the USA whence he issued barbs against American capitalism. But in spite of the more specific renewed attacks on Jewish writers during Stalin's last years, he survived successfully.

His journalistic daily reports published originally in *Soviet War News* and collected under the title *Russia at War* (1943) are instructive. They are his reactions to figures and events in Germany in particular and to the war in general, from July 1941 until July 1942. This is a hard hitting, unambiguous, unanalytical, trenchant attack on Nazism, naturally in accord with the Soviet line. He speaks as a true believer: 'We are attacking because we have on our side humanity, truth, the wisdom of history and the sweetness of that little fair-haired girl who is waving her hand in welcome to the Red Star and calling out over and over again "It's our people! It's our people!" ' But if the cold truth is a major consideration, then there are some odd omissions. He writes: 'When Hitler was preparing to attack Russia, he kept silent. He made no boast of the number of divisions that had been sent to the Russian frontier, nor did he breath a word about when or where he intended to move.' This would be the natural context for a mention of the Nazi-Soviet pact, which he could then complain had been breached. But of course the Soviets are constantly revising history in the light of the latest policy. And after Hitler had attacked the Soviet Union, the pact which had been initiated by Stalin (Hitler's statement had been printed in *Pravda*) no longer existed. Nor was it even on record as having once been in existence.

The Jews are also almost entirely absent in Ehrenburg's account. He writes: 'The S.S. became jailers in the concentration camps, they headed punitive detachments in the subjugated countries, and were the sworn tormentors of French, Poles, Norwegians and Serbs.' So these for the author, are the prime targets of Nazi hatred! What we know of Nazi preoccupations suggests something different. But the official Soviet historiography reduces and sometimes even nullifies the Jewish presence. Even with Nazism, the Jews may not be accounted special victims, or even victims on an equal footing. Nazis are known as Hitlerites and capitalists and, from 1941 onwards, as anti-Socialists. The leader of the fight against Nazism is the glorious Soviet Union. Ehrenburg even suggests that the Allies are not pulling their weight sufficiently in the common struggle. He does not trouble to mention that the USSR are only in the struggle at all because they were directly attacked. And that was long after the Allies had been embroiled. Soviet society is still the greatest for him. 'We can say without boasting that in many spheres our nation has outstripped the others. We love the future. It is the breath of our life.' And later: 'Soviet people never, never, never shall be slaves!'

That the Soviet people were never slaves is disputed by accounts of what actually transpired there. Evgenia Ginzburg (b. 1907), a self-styled Leninist Communist, tells in *Into the Whirlwind* (1967) of her horrific experience — eighteen years in prison and labour camps for no particular reason. As she was 'rehabilitated' with many others in 1956, she can perhaps afford to regard Stalinism as a transient aberration to be subsumed under the heading 'cult of personality'. It is, for her, something that 'was and never shall be again'. She seems to rejoice in the situation that it is now 'possible to tell everyone about what happened'. Only her account was never published in the USSR. It had to be smuggled out for initial publication in Milan. Her accounts of the Terror sounds convincing and confirms other reports. For her, 1934 is the beginning of that period which reached its climax with the show trials of 1936 and 1937. At that earlier stage, she says of herself: 'I had not the slightest doubt that the party line was right.' Her only reservation turned on the personality of Stalin himself, whom she refused to hold in reverence. Others, even those convicted arbitrarily 'managed strangely to combine a sane judgement of what was going on in the country with a truly mystical personal cult of Stalin'. She does not see the irony in the rejection of Stalinism for Leninism, even though Lenin set up the system under which she suffered so terribly. But her account does assert human values, the centrality of the individual, the value of poetry, and does provide an abundance of information. But the 'system' that tortured and enslaved people and suppressed free expression both predated Stalin and survived him. Mandelstam, Pasternak, Babel, Solzhenitsyn and Ginzburg herself (to name but a very few examples) are published and read in the world outside, not in the Soviet Union. The effects of Kruschev's 'secret speech' of 1956 and the collective rehabilitation were not radical.

This summary then has to take into account the arbitrariness of the machine and its haphazard results. We have to be thankful that in spite of all, so much has been published either locally or abroad, and that such an abundance of quality has survived. The Jewish contribution is manifest, always curbed, sometimes repressed, unexpectedly accepted for short periods, and ambivalently problematic. One of the greatest works of Soviet humour *The Twelve Chairs* (1928) was co-authored by a Jew, Ilya Ilf (1897-1937) together with Yevgeni Petrov (1903-1942). Ilf also originated from that resource centre of Jewish culture, Odessa, and introduces a wealth of Jewish folklore into his tale of the unscrupulous scoundrel Ostap Bender. Bender says: 'No-one likes us, except for the Criminal Investigation Department which doesn't like us either.' And he writes an imaginary obituary of himself: 'He loved and suffered. He loved money and suffered from a lack of it.' The humour is grotesque as the plot takes unexpected turns in an essentially improbably direction. The two heroes (Bender is roped in by the nephew, pathetic instigator of the action) are determined to locate the twelve chairs of an aunt's estate which had been whisked away, and in one of which a fortune's worth of jewellery was secreted. This takes them on many adventures all over Russia. And when they come to the final chair, they discover that the contents have already been removed and the proceeds disbursed to finance a club for workers. In the immediate post-Stalin euphoria of 'the thaw' (a term coined by Ehrenburg), this work was reprinted in an edition of 200,000 copies.

Otherwise, most works, including anti-Stalinist material (in spite of the official destalinisation) are published abroad. *The Trial Begins* (1960) by Abram Tertz, otherwise known as Andrey Sinyavsky (b. 1925) attacks the anti-Semitism of Stalin's last years. The events of this amusing and grotesque account, also in the tradition of Gogol and Ilf and Petrov, take place just before the Leader's death, and revolve around the nonsensical but horrifying so-called 'Doctors' Plot'. It is said of the Jews there that 'every schoolboy knew today that these people with their petty bourgeois instincts were born enemies of socialism, homeless cosmopolitans'. This is not just a parody but a true representation of Stalinist terminology. The novel has 'Brave New World' elements. The Authorities see enemies everywhere. Eventually, the death of the 'Master' brings about a modification of the processes, but they forget to release Rabinovich, a doctor who was imprisoned through Stalinist paranoia. This is a recognition that the situation was not essentially altered on Stalin's demise.

Tertz is not Jewish, but he is closely associated with a Jewish translator Yuli Daniel. Both were tried in 1966 for having published slanderous and subversive works abroad (Labedz and Hayward), and in 1973, allowed to emigrate. We are witnessing a continuation of the tradition of Soviet *émigré* literature, a literature in the great line of the Russian tradition. Pre-soviet concerns are still alive — Russian humanism and the rays from that nineteenth-century Enlightenment. We also have many illuminating beams cast on the Jewish question in this work.

5 HEBREW LITERATURE BETWEEN EXILE AND HOME

There is a continuous tradition of Hebrew literature from the Bible to the present day. Hebrew is coterminous with the Jewish people, whose writers have used it uninterruptedly as a major language and usually as the principal external and 'sacred' language. But because of its largely sacred associations with the Bible and its commentaries, with liturgy and holy poetry, with Jewish law and love, it did not easily absorb secular material. Of course, there was such. Even the so-called sacred literature has secular elements. And medieval writers had also prided themselves on their ability to adapt the tongue to every form of literary expression. Nevertheless, in the post-medieval phase, and particularly in Eastern Europe where the largest Jewish communities resided, Hebrew was more and more separated off into a special compartment.

That is, until the period of Enlightenment. From the late eighteenth century and particularly in the nineteenth, one of the objects of the enlighteners had been to revive a Hebrew literary tradition in all its facets and to use it as a vehicle for contemporary literature in its finest and most developed expression. They wanted to write essays, pamphlets, stories, novels and poetry of all kinds (not just religious) in Hebrew by adapting the ancient source material into a new mould. It was not the cause but the effect that there was a rupture in the Hebrew literary tradition. The writers who preceded this rupture were rooted in a traditional understanding of Jewish peoplehood and God's commandments, and those who followed it sought truth, wisdom and beauty wherever. This was the condition of the Jew in the nineteenth century in general. The breach was only more evident in Hebrew because of the nature of the transformation, because of the way that the very words were now used in a different sense. The Hebrew language was the most sensitive barometer to the nature of the Jewish revolution in modern times.

The greatest of the Hebrew writers were those who were aware of what happened, and could register its drama on their own person. They sought substitutes for the lost certainties, sometimes one in secular nationalism or in theories of emancipation. No-one more expressed a sense of tragic loss than H. N. Bialik (1865-1934), born and reared in Volhynia, within the Pale of Settlement, where by 1897 there were more than five million Jews (Gilbert). The lingua franca was Yiddish, but the cultural elite cultivated Hebrew. A bilingual literature was produced (see Chapter 1), very often by bilingual writers. Bialik was one such, but he tended, particularly in his later development, more to Hebrew, and it is in this language that he expressed his invincible sense of loss and search, national striving and personal grief.

Ironic indeed is the fact that this very private and lyrical writer has been labelled 'National poet' and even 'prophet'. It is easier to sense the common denominator of his mood than to locate the source of distress. For a national poet, his sentiments are paradoxical and ultimately mysterious. But his achievement is to marry the public and private theme, so to self-identify with the national situation that he becomes its source of public expression, even though the object of expression is locked in his own ego. From his first poem 'El Hatzipor' ('To the Bird') written at the age of eighteen, he writes in an already established 'Hibat Zion' ('Love of Zion') tradition of his longing for the Holy Land and the sufferings of the people. But his own suffering, even within that convention, turns into the dominant theme, so that poet and nation become one. He can write poems which were adopted as national hymns, inviting his readership's enthusiastic participation in the re-establishment of the people amidst a sorry scene of national disintegration, physical and spiritual. But he can also write of his own defection in such a way as to suggest that this too is the general condition. He expressed a generation that lost its traditional faith, its ancient anchor, its certainty, and strayed off on new paths. The conclusion to his famour poem 'Hamathmid' ('The Persistent Scholar'), after a portrayal of the devoted Talmudist which he himself had once been, goes: 'I have left my Torah, I have sinned for bread,/ And have got lost on another path.'

The poet has strayed. This is one of the basic data of the situation. But the other datum is more problematic: 'He will never be free of the image of his background' (Yudkin), so he will always carry within himself the memory of the path from which he has strayed. He will never be able to embrace a new direction with enthusiasm, but will always be mourning the necessary loss of a dear departed. Still the search continued. He is aware that he has missed out on a very precious element, love, whose climax is death. In the poem 'Tziporeth' ('Butterfly'), 1904, he combines the elements of love and adventure:

'Hurry, hurry, my sister, let us go back to the forest,
Where under the canopy of the groves I will take out all my soul.
And with all my love which hangs on a hair
Let us put ourselves to death with a kiss.'

Images of death are as constant in Bialik's poetry as the images of love with which they are combined. There is a suggestion that ultimate fulfilment is only possible beyond the threshold. He remains loyal to a tradition which is no longer alive, as in 'Lifne aron hasfarim' ('Before the Bookcase'), 1910, where that powerful weight of the past is seen to be on the point of collapse:

'I saw my fortress, and it was broken down,
And I saw the Shekhinah leaving its place,
. . . The flame of my candle alone was still sputtering
And it moved leaping in death throes,
When suddenly the window burst open and all was extinguished.'

But what of the poet amongst this devastation?

'And I, a tender chick, cast from its nest,
Am left in night and its darkness.'

He does not leave for newer pastures. He is part of the devastation itself. That life has crumbled around him in two respects. Physically, poverty, pogroms and emigration have eaten away at the communities. Spiritually, Jews have simply lost their old confidence in a set of values that seemed permanent. Our poet has totally self-identified with the situation.

But he goes beyond that too. The implication of this stance is an insistence on a light that will never shine and on a truth that will never emerge. Except 'after death'. Bialik, in his poem entitled 'Aharey mothiy' ('After my death'), 1904, writes his own obituary. His 'Poetry' had always yearned for a particular note:

'Silently moved, silently trembled,
Towards its song, its lover, its redeemer.
It yearned, thirsted, ached, longed
. . . But it tarried and did not come.'

And in one of his last poems, 'Hetzitz Wameth' ('He Peeped and Died'), 1917, he images one striving to attain the fiftieth gate, the one which, according to Rabbinic legend was beyond Moses himself, the 'greatest of the people'. His ambition apparently knows no bounds. But the conclusion is:

'Then the torch is extinguished, the doors of the gate open
And he peeps inside.
Then his corpse sank down, by its side a smoking reed, crouched
Over the threshold of nothingness.'

This is remarkably similar to the tale told in Kafka's *The Trial* where death intervenes at the moment of realisation.

The hero of Bialik's poetry is the poet himself, who appears time and again as the lonely searcher doomed to disappointment. His own biography parallels his literature. He cut short his central literary work early in his life, imposing a tight-lipped silence on his muse. Instead, he devoted himself to editorial activity and to anthologising national literary treasures, Rabbinic, medieval and modern. With his arrival in Palestine in 1924, a further nail was knocked in the coffin of diaspora Hebrew literature. It is the 1920s that marked the transfer of the Hebrew literary centre to Eretz Yisrael. The diaspora was to be squeezed out by the forces of communism in the Soviet Union, assimilation and unilingualism in America, and then physically by the holocaust of two decades later. Hebrew was cultivated extensively only by the yishuv (i.e. Jewish settlement in Palestine) which was increasing in force and numbers. Hebrew was now the official language of this small but dedicated kernel of special souls, and it was to become the instrument of statehood. As a consequence, the type of literature produced changed. Hebrew, the literary language, was now also the vernacular, a mother tongue for increasing numbers, a common workaday tool, not a particular special service tongue. Bialik had noted a move from sacralism to secularism of which he was a part. That old world was to die, and he offered its eulogy together with his own.

It is in the nature of the situation outlined that many Hebrew writers would bestride the two worlds of Israel and diaspora. These two elements are not only separate geographically, they are also two worlds in space, in time, in history. S. Y. Agnon (1888-1970) commented on each through the other. As a storyteller, he brought to the reader a cultivated awareness of Rabbinic legend, ancient and modern, of the truly faithful Hasid both in his origins and in the modern world. But he crossed the two worlds, and gave Hebrew fiction its most sophisticated technical equipment in creating a multi-layered form of story, novella and novel in the European manner. Born in Buczacz, Galicia, having emigrated to Palestine twice and lived in Berlin in the interim, he also was familiar with the Jewish heritage and its recent fate the world over.

Like Bialik in poetry, Agnon was a master of counterpoint, contrasting not only the past with the present, but the world of faith with the world from which it is absent. Although the author himself is orthoprax and creates a Rabbinic context by the use of a range of sources, it would be wrong to assume that the overall burden of his narrative offers an unambiguous message. On the contrary, his tales of faith are deeply ambivalent, as his psychological narrative often conveys the opposite lesson from the one expected. This may also too readily assume a didacticism, but the reader is surely tempted into drawing conclusions from the mysteries on offer. Where we expect saintliness to be recorded, suffering seems to follow. When it is a leap of faith in the direction of a return to the world of tradition, disaster can ensue.

Agnon seems to adopt two quite separate modes of writing. One is narrative from within the situation of faith, in which no criticism is offered and the narrator could be one of the 'community of the pious'. The other has a less defined 'narrated' context (it could be European or Palestinian), and the narrative voice presents the events from the outside in the way that the omniscient narrator does. There can be a mixture, as when the narrator seems to be wholly trusting, but where the turn of events is so odd that the narrative comments on itself, and the unfolding plot expresses its own doubts on the narrator's credibility. But the author is not schizophrenic. The modes themselves, so different in their approaches, illuminate each other, as does the author's practice of contrasting worlds and outlooks. And it may be that the Agnon here is not so localised in time and space as might appear. Perhaps he himself crosses the barriers in a world out of time: 'For all the profound historicity of the Judaic vision of the world, these people lack the poignant sense of time that we inherit from the Judaeo-Christian tradition' (Hochman).

Not all Agnon's stories in the Hasidic mode conclude in misfortune. A well-known novella, *Bilevav Yamim (In the Heart of the Seas)*, 1935, tells of one Hananiah, a man of perfect faith, who achieves the aim set for himself, viz. to reach Palestine. There are many obstacles to be overcome en route, as is indeed inevitable. Living in Israel is so central to the faith, that Satan must do his utmost to prevent divine intervention; and a miracle enables him to reach Israel before anyone else. Is there a moral here? The lesson seems so obvious as to preclude amplification. But the author himself provides a cautionary note at the end: 'There are those who will read the book as one reading legends. And there are those readers who will receive some benefit for themselves. About the first I quote (Proverbs 12) "A good thing will

make it glad, a good thing gladdens the soul and saves from worry",
and about the latter I quote (Psalms 37) "And those who hope for God
will inherit the earth".' So there are two possible sorts of reader. The
one who reads purely for pleasure and the other who reads for moral
instruction. Both types are legitimate and each may find satisfaction in
a different way. But probably, as the author is doubtless aware, the
typical modern reader falls into neither category. He is too sceptical to
be carried away by the story, and too morally blunted to seek
instruction in a story. The author has protected himself *ab initio* from a
failure to achieve these targets by incorporating the implied criticism.
And he can even revenge himself on the flawed reader before that
criticism is voiced.

Agnon's other mode is probably more accessible to the modern
reader. His assured place in Hebrew literature derives, to a large extent,
like Bialik's, from the way that he has summed up a national mood and
expressed it as a personal truth. In his apposition of contrasts, the
author has etched a dying civilisation. He bore witness to the physical
and spiritual decay in the sources of Judaism. After he settled
permanently in Palestine in 1924, he made one more return visit to his
home town in 1930, a visit which constitutes the subject matter for his
novel, *Oreah Natah Lalun (Guest for the Night)*. His home town
Buczacz appears under the name Shibosh (a play on a Hebrew root
meaning to spoil), and he describes a scene of physical degradation in
the community which has palpably disintegrated. Even the very few
Jews who constitute the tiny residue of local Jewry have lost their
faith in divine providence, and merely go through the motions of
keeping up the now almost disused synagogue. They are only too
happy to surrender the key to the guest, who is the only one interested
in the welfare of that institution.

A different sort of encounter takes place in a later novel, *Thmol
Shilshom (Yesteryear)*, which is set in Palestine, and tells of one
Yitzhak Kumer who 'left his land, his birthplace and his city and went
up to the land of Israel, to raise it from its desolation and to be built
up by it'. We see that the move from country to country expresses not
only a historical fact, but also a hope of spiritual regeneration. The
suggestion is that the old world of the stetl is dead, and that there is
some possibility of meaningful survival in the Holy land, where the
reconstruction is to take place. But, as in Brenner's Palestinian stories,
the new reality is by no means rosy. The immigrants have not managed
to submerge their own personal temperaments, ambitions and
frustrations in the national effort. Religion here too is narrow and

intolerant. Kumer hovers between two worlds, the secular and the secred. He first makes his home in Jaffa, where he lives a life far removed from what his traditional upbringing would suggest. But the magnet of Jerusalem draws his old loyalty. He is also prepared to surrender his Jaffa lady Sonia to merit the pious Shifra. But a mad dog, Balak, stalks Jerusalem, terrifying everyone. Balak, it seems, is a thinking dog which must be exterminated. Kumer, in his encounter with the mad dog, is bitten and dies. This surrealistic imagery sets the two worlds now not only in contrast but in violent opposition to each other. Only one can survive in the fight to the death, exclusivist tradition or free thought. But you are liable to be bitten by this free-ranging spirit if you attempt to return too late. No simple lesson emerges. The return that Kumer assays is unfortunately inorganic, and the mad dog is already within him.

The author's central preoccupation is with the way that unrecognised, unconscious forces gradually take control of the personality, turning it in directions rejected by the conscious mind and the super ego. In a posthumous novel, *Shirah,* this force is expressed in the form of a nurse who makes only a brief appearance early on, but whose psychical presence holds all of Herbst's attention. Herbst had spent the night of his baby's birth with Shirah, but for all his attempts to rectify his stance, he cannot free himself from her negative fascination. Conscience is outflanked by the unconscious. He is disturbed in his family life and in his academic work. So many of Agnon's tales indeed revolve around intention frustrated. The individual is indeed divided into good and evil inclination. But the good cannot win out merely by being invoked. The plots of Agnon's stories parallel the structure of the psyche. Shirah is like the unconscious, practically invisible in the action, but dominant in practice. These factors are richly suggestive for the nation as well as for individuals. All sorts of unseen forces are at work, and these may take over in spite of the deliberate and rational selection of other alternatives.

Hebrew literature had, as we observed, become concentrated in the Yishuv by the 1920s. The large-scale immigration in the wake of the Great War is known as the third wave (aliyah). It was this wave that really established the community as a permanent factor in the mandated territory, and set the secure foundation for a State in the making. It marked the transition from a creative diaspora now in decline to a last-ditch stand for the retention of authentic Jewish existence. This wave more than doubled the existing settlement, although the peak year of the decade for immigration was 1925, in the wave following, when 34,000 came (Bein). The country was being transformed. Collective settlements were established and new towns set up. By 1931, the Jewish population of Palestine was 174,610 (Patai). This is a small number in terms of the world Jewish population but it does represent a vast increase, and the new immigration, particularly in the first half of the 1920s was not a cross-section of the overall pululation, but largely agricultural, male, young and impoverished (Laqueur).

The generation of writers that was reaching maturity at this time brought to Hebrew literature two things: (1) an awareness of European experience, of the horror, the degradation, the disintegration of Jewry and a knowledge of how literature was reacting; and (2) a pioneering enthusiasm for the new Palestinian experience which could also be transmuted into literature. The most distinctive contribution was in poetry, where writers such as Y. Karni (1884-1949), A. Shlonsky (1900-73), Y. Lamdan (1900-54), N. Alterman (1910-73) and U. Z. Greenberg (1894-1981) were consciously creating a new Hebrew poetics. Shlonsky, in particular, saw himself as an iconoclast, lambasting the 'generation of Bialik', and arguing the case for an appropriate experimental vanguard in the new circumstances. A changing situation should produce revolutionary literature. In Europe, Expressionism and Futurism had emerged from the war. (We have already noted that in fact their origins predate the war, but they became widely popular and characteristic afterwards.) Language had changed, metre had changed, subject matter had changed.

Most innovative of all the poets, and the one whose contribution is probably also the most permanent, was U. Z. Greenberg, originally from Eastern Galicia, spending a period in Warsaw and Berlin after the war, and emigrating to Palestine in 1924. He had belonged to a Yiddish Expressionist vanguard, fulminating in poetry and prose on the need for a full-blooded Jewish literature. His move to Palestine also marked his changeover to Hebrew writing. He transferred European Expression to Hebrew literature, demanding an appropriate response to the violence of the era and the experiment in national revival now taking place. The vision had to be brought back to Jewish life and the fire to its literature. He attacks the notion of 'art for art's sake' in favour of an art in service of the people. Bialik, he says, had once roared like a lion, and we need a Bialik for the current era. Or, to invoke a poet of another nation, we need a Walt Whitman of our own. Shlonsky had appropriated Russian revolutionary doctrine for a Hebrew verse, reflecting the pioneering nature of the Hebrew revolution. Greenberg looks for his models as much to the ancient past as to the present, to Ezekiel, prophet of return and national reconstruction. If Mayakovsky was the model for one, with his daring neologisms and his anti-authoritarianism, the Bible, opus to the people at the time of its greatness, was the model for the second. Like the ancient prophets, Greenberg castigates the people, accusing them of betraying ideals, trivialising and desecrating everything holy. In his first Hebrew volume, *Eymah Gdolah Weyareah (Great Dread and Moon),* he notes that although the time is ripe, no prophet has arisen to give the people direction: 'The face of the generation is that of a dog. Messianic days without Messiah. Impudence is great. My God, my father, a goat has gone into the palaces.' There is a potential 'kingdom arising out of the desert of El-Arish towards Damascus – the golden document is still preserved; David's conquest is still called a conquest.' The people here are building oracles to the sun. And the poet states his own function: 'I am a poor man like you. But I will sing to your labours.' The task of the Hebrew poet in the contemporary context is to articulate the people's struggle.

One of Greenberg's principal subjects is the function of the poet. He celebrates his own thirtieth birthday with an invitation issued to himself, as it were, by others, those 'generations sunk in their aching flesh and blood'. They command the grandson (himself):

'Arise, express us, living man!
Do not sing of the splendour of heaven, speak of man living on earth.
Flesh, blood, water, house, implements'

> *(Hagavruth Haolah, Rising Manhood).*

He brings confirmation now of the message that he received thirty years before soon after he was born, when he was so hurt in the name of Judaism 'during the circumcision rite'. Like Bialik and Agnon, Greenberg synthesises public and personal pain, and makes of them a unity, each expressing the other. The pain of the nation and the pain of the individual come together in circumcision. The nation's torment at its loss of land, the poet's grief at the loss of mother are parallel. Man is born to loneliness and suffering. In the *Anaqreon* cycle, he receives his own pessimistic answer:

'What is joy? – Ascent
For the purpose of a deep descent
More powerful into sadness.'

Men have lost their beliefs, the nation has lost its hold. The individual has lost his root in the soil which is his home. All of these images express the central fact of homelessness and the search for restoration.

Many observers have noted a persistent sense of orphanhood in modern Hebrew literature. This is only to be expected. The conditions of the production of this literature were peculiar. There can be few cases similar to the circumstances of its birth. In character, it was revolutionary, standing the tradition on its head, reversing the inherited values and emptying the vessel (Hebrew) of its old contents, and then struggling to find something new. This was a historical breach, as there was a breach too in geographical continuity. As the literature was severed from the past, only related in estrangement, so the land of Israel was physically separated from the familiar landscape of diaspora. So many Hebrew writers of the period expressed dislocation. For Greenberg, this was a constant theme. In a late sequence of poems, from the volume *Rehovoth Hanahar (Streets of the River)* mainly reacting to the European holocaust, the poet's world is broken. He is, by virtue of being mortal, doomed 'to die in the valley'. His mother is not present at that point. The father is there, but he is God, frightening and angry. Father and mother are two opposed principles, comfort and rebuke. Life is a progress from a peak to the valley, a constant descent. Just when he needs succour from its sole source, the mother has gone:

'On the topmost peak: joy
Born is man,
On the topmost peak: joy,
The cradle stands.

At that point, everything is well and offers support to the baby in the cradle. But then when childhood days pass, this 'ladder melts away'. This is the ladder that in Jacob's dream connected Heaven with Earth, enabling God to reach man through his agents, the angels. Mature man no longer has this connection. He is alone. And then comes his time to die:

'But man does not die on the peak:
Man leaves the cradle to grow into the valley.
Man dies in the valley and above him is time
The body is so sad and lonely!
He needs his mother then exceedingly!

And the mother is not in the valley!
Night descends on her son.'

Instead of revelling in achievement, man becomes increasingly estranged and isolated. The one thing that does remain is the sense of duty, the father principle God, demanding, exacting and ultimately mysterious. But this is the principle that will survive the individual, the son. It is beyond human transience.

Greenberg's enormous output, extending over seventy years, evinces a remarkable unity through the diversity of form and overt subject matter. The separate elements – the personal, the national and the religious – merge into one block grasped by the individual poet. This formidable writing will not easily tolerate imitators. A false note in the orchestration reduces the overall sense to bombast. But the work does have its own controlled consistency. A mythology emerges. Jewish history continues, its destiny marked out since Sinai. God demands, and the people must respond appropriately. The present time is awesome in the delicate implications of that response. The poet has a special function as a spokesman of the people, but also as a prophet to them. But as a mortal he, unfortunately, can only expect death without the comfort of a mother, sole shield against disaster.

Hebrew fiction between the wars, with the exception of Agnon's work, is not as experimental as the poetry. It used the forms and innovations that had been established by the previous generations. H. Hazaz (1898-1972), for example, adapted the language and manner of his predecessors for his prose, to erect a monument to the Jewry of the past to describe the communities of the present. Born in the Ukraine, he moved to Paris in 1921, and then settled in Palestine in 1931. He started to write at the end of the Great War, but his major works really emerged from the 1930s onwards, and were often revised in the course of republication and production of new editions.

As is the case with Agnon, Hazaz's writing, at first glance, seems to reflect very separate concerns and to treat them differently. On the one hand, diaspora, on the other, Israel. In one stratum, the Yemenites, both in their original homeland and in Palestine; in the other, the more sophisticated European communities, past and present. But a closer examination does after all reveal a single thread running through – an obsession with the Jew and his history. His stories, long and short, early and late, as well as his play and his speeches (some of which were collected and published posthumously) revolve around the meaning of

Jewish history. But for the author, this Jewish situation is capable of change, and the agent of change, certainly for earlier generations and for some elements in the contemporary world, is the Messiah. The one play that Hazaz wrote, *Beqetz Hayamim (At the End of Days)*, 1935, is about Messianic expectation, set in Germany at the time of Shabatay Tzevi. Western Jewry once held this faith in the imminence of the Messiah. Eastern Jewry is still in possession of it. A neat contrast is often drawn in those of Hazaz's stories where the two types of Jew are set side by side. Because now, the Western Jew no longer believes in an external miraculous agent of change, although he might think that people could affect the course of history, and move it in a different direction.

All Hazaz's writing is motivated by this interest, seeking understanding. Although he is rooted in the tradition of the Enlightenment, and is particularly influenced in his language and approach by Mendeli, the author is not critical in accordance with that tradition. He is fully in sympathy with his subject. Perhaps he can afford to be since the world of the stetl that he sometimes describes is now dead. He is not engaged in a polemic on those grounds. He seeks to recall. In a story called 'Early Generations' in *Rehayim Shevurim (Broken Mill)*, 1942, he opens: 'Beloved by me are the hamlets of yesteryear, poor homes of the Jewish community, condemned by generations of writers and commentators, undermined by poetasters and rhymesters, mocked by fools and cleverdicks, enslaved by governments and administrators, breached by bands of brigands and robbers, until they have finally disappeared.' The subject of the author's dirge is much lamented. And it does not relate to only one particular area or community. He is talking really about East-European Jewry in general, the culture of the Pale of Settlement which has now disappeared as an organised element and no longer has the cohesion of a people. Unlike Mendeli and the other satirists, Hazaz remembers all with affection. ('Remembers' is the operative word; he cannot see it any more). He includes in this affection traits that would have been scorned by the said 'writers and commentators' such as otherworldliness and faith. In another story he writes: 'It sometimes happens to a Jew that he has had a surfeit of the world's vanities, and cleaves to the Creator in holiness, enthusiasm and devotion.' This is clearly said out of affection, not in criticism, in a spirit of understanding for a Jewish pietism that transcends mediocrity and practicality. Hazaz is insistent when he deals with a specific case on its relation to the general and on its typicality.

This concern with Jewish history and with Messianism as the force of change obviously has implications for the present and for the author's understanding of current events in Israel. 'Redemption' is something that is actually taking place in Palestine/Israel. Many have regarded the tribulations of the Holocaust and the Arab-Israeli war as the first phase, 'the beginning of redemption'. The author can both illustrate his attitude to Jewish history and his contrast of the two communities in stories that juxtapose the two. Such is 'Rahamim' which, like so many of the author's stories, does not contain a developed plot so much as the germ of a situation and the expression of character contrasts. It is simply a meeting of two individuals. One, Menashke, is thin, sickly and tired, and feels himself a failure in all respects. He is not at peace in the world, and is not only personally frustrated, but also generally resentful of external elements. The other, who chances upon him in Jerusalem, presents a very different picture, contented though impoverished as he straddles his ass. They seem to come not only from different eras. Rahamim the Kurd (as he turns out to be) is very forthcoming and, in his primitive Hebrew, offers practical advice to the other. He must get married. As much as Rahamim reveals himself so does Mendeli conceal himself (although the author does permit glimpses of an unhappy past). Each character, in fact, sees into the other's life. Rahamim tells how he got to Palestine. Menashke, through his demeanour and his limited conversation, hints at the source of his misery. Rahamim goes his own way, after repeating his advice about marriage, but then returns to offer consolation: ' "God will have mercy." ' Menashke's mood changes only through recall of Rahamim's smile. Perhaps the price of sophistication and high expectation is discontent.

And there is a similar though more sustained juxtaposition of types in the late novel *Beqolar Ehad (In One Noose)*, 1963. This is set in Palestine during the last days of British mandatory rule, when the Jewish nationalist movements, in their efforts to remove the rulers, wage war against them. Two men under sentence of death await execution in their cell, Menahem Halperin of the Irgun and Eliyahu Mizrahi of Lehi. However disparate their background, their object is identical. Specifically, they had the same consciousness of the vitality and relevance of Jewish history, which, for them, was still operative: 'Those far-off things which happened thousands of years ago were nearer to them than things which happened within their parents' lifetime a generation earlier.' But the same sort of contrast is observable here as in 'Rahamim'. Eliyahu the Oriental is at ease with himself, whereas Menahem is melancholy. Again, there is the contrast between the two world views, the naive and the sentimental. These are two representative types of Jew, both, in the author's view, acting authentically and arriving at a single conclusion expressed in action. But the European is uneasy, unhappy, full of dread. The Oriental is distinguished by a tranquil acceptance of his role. Menahem recognises that he has lost that total faith, and is therefore estranged from his community. The process of distancing that began with the Enlightenment is still working itself out here on the current scene. Menahem is angry with himself, with the Jews for adopting a passive stance and for rejecting redemption. The Jew's characteristic posture, he argues, is that of Isaac awaiting slaughter. That will never change. But Eliyahu believes that change is possible. Fate has the shape of the will. And, in fact, the plot supports Eliyahu's view. The two take their fate into their own hands, and blow themselves up in their cell before the execution can take place. They have deprived the British of a victim, and they have acted freely and authentically. Even in death, however, the two remain different. Eliyahu's countenance bears the marks of repose, whereas Menahem's is disturbed.

The author constantly raises the views of free will and determinism as opposed ways of understanding Jewish history. Are Jews the subject of history or its object? Characters in the stories, such as Yudka in 'The Sermon', suggest that Jewish history is not history at all in any dynamic sense. History is made by an active agent which imposes its will on events. Jewish 'history' is not of this nature. The Jews have been on the receiving end in all circumstances, places and periods since the Exile. And this Exile has become so deeply rooted in the Jewish character that it has become integral to it. Jews now, unconsciously of course, like their role. In 'The Sermon', Yudka's speech is just one element in the story, so no easy substitution can be made between Yudka's stance and that of the author. The author of a fiction is rightly a master of disguise. A story is not in itself a sermon. Hazaz has raised the subjects and terms of reference, within which the debate can take place. Obviously, an attitude does emerge, but it is within the context of a dialectic.

The Hebrew tale is as old as the Bible itself. Men have always related the fortunes of themselves and of others, of their adventures, of their development and of the way that they have become what they are. The Bible opens with an account of the origins of the world, of the first people on Earth, of the struggle between God and man, between right and wrong. Medieval Hebrew literature too revelled in the moral tale, often told in Spain, in the Arabic-type magama of rhymed prose. And in post-Renaissance times too, many novelists have set the tale at the heart of their work, even if it has become a subsidiary element in modern prose.

Such a writer is the Jerusalem-born Hebrew fictionist, Yehuda Burla (1886-1969), who was productive for about half a century from the outbreak of the Great War. Prose writers have to a great extent reappraised form and matter, have evidenced scepticism in regard to character and plot, and have thus sensed a need for formal innovation. But Burla has persisted throughout with the traditional tale about men and women perceived as 'characters' affected by life's circumstances and changing in respect to those circumstances. Burla's novels always have a hero at the centre. This hero is placed in a setting which arouses conflict, and the conflict is often between his inclination and his environment. Events occur which proceed from the conflict and influence the hero on life's journey. And the climax, whether disastrous as in *Aliloth Aqavyah (Aqavyah's Deeds),* 1939, or conciliatory, as in *Naftuley Adam (Man's Struggle* published in English as *In Darkness Striving*), 1928, points up the conflict within the individual described. And the tale is told in the traditional picaresque manner.

Burla's writing is out of step with its time and provenance. Hebrew prose had become experimental in the early part of the century, adapting the lessons of psychology to new forms of narrative and language. Character was not now to be observed just from the outside, but felt from within and expressed with a lack of certainty in awareness of psychological waves (stream of consciousness). Notions of good and evil became muddied in uncertainty and borderline recognition of mixed motives. Burla's work in form belongs to an earlier era. In subject matter too, Burla's material was largely unfamiliar to the Hebrew reader – the Arabic or Ladino speaking hero without intellectual sophistication, the observant Jew from an Islamic environment, the social assumptions of the Orient (as regards the place of woman, for example).

The Burla story typically plunges straight into the action and the central theme, e.g. sexual desire in the face of society's constraints. Even when the desire appears to be fulfilled, some breach of social norms (even if minor) exacts its vengeance. Burla's very first story 'Luna' (written in 1914 but published only after the war) is a case in point. Here, the brother of a deceased landlord comes to Jurusalem to see his property. One of his tenants, a nubile girl, attracts the attention of the older married man. He, Obadiah, argues that monogamy is not a typically Jewish practice, but rather a debased Ashkenazi custom, imitative of the European. He, as a Sephardi (Bucharan, in his case), can ignore the convention and take a new wife. This he fully expects to effect his revitalisation. His motivation is clear. His life has turned stale, but he is as libidinous as ever, and would like nothing more than legitimate fulfilment. What, though, is Luna's motivation? She, at twenty-four, thinks that life has already passed her by, and feels 'like someone seeing his friend suck something sour in his palate, whilst his own mouth remains empty. His soul is empty, empty yet demanding.' She is fatherless, and her impoverished mother can offer no dowry. So the inevitable marriage takes place, and disaster immediately ensues. Obadiah turns out to be not as wealthy as was thought and, more importantly, is mean and inconsiderate. Hitherto, Luna had been unfulfilled, but now she is desolate because there is no prospect of improvement. She has a father rather than a husband, and a very unpleasant father at that. He too is disappointed, with her arrogance and irritation. They have to split up, especially as his first wife suddenly makes an appearance. Even though she is pregnant when the separation is planned, Luna feels victorious and trustful in the future.

This plot illustrates some of the author's preoccupations. The social context is Oriental, but within that blanket term are contained divisions. He is a long-standing Palestinian of Bucharan origin, and she is newly arrived from Istanbul (Ladino speaking and of higher social status). In spite of what appears to be a propitious basis for a marriage that should extend advantages to both parties, the seeds of conflict are sown at the outset. Their expectations are as disparate as their ages. He seeks respect and loyalty, she romance and excitement. His ways are set, her life is just starting. So with the difference of perspective emerge disruption and disaster. The plot could be summarised as two expectations unfulfilled. Both are based on actual, current, psychological need. But this need drives out wider considerations, long term, social and communal. The broader context then mitigates against the action taken by the individual in his search for immediate satisfaction. Such is the nature of the Burla story, based on the data of: (1) inherent character; (2) dissatisfaction; (3) search; (4) solution; (5) retribution; and (6) crisis. Of course, not all the ingredients appear in all the stories. The plots are as different as their settings. But we do always get a development of this sort. The Burla story is of character in action. The time scale is often large (a lifetime of many decades can be covered), the setting moves (Syria, Iraq, Anatolia, Palestine — country, town), the hero is of various hues – vicious, as in *Ishto Hasnuah (His Hated Wife)*, 1925, adventurous, as in *Aliloth Aqavyah*, simple as in *Beliy Kokhav (Without a Star)*, 1927, sophisticated as in *Naftuley Adam;* but he is always perceived in this narrative manner. The work moves along these stages, although the resolution may diverge. This resolution emerges from the conflict between character and the resistant force within the context of the plot.

It is character that is basic to the Burla story, character perceived, drawn, invoked, described. The heroes of the novels are variations on each other, varying in appearance, apparent temperament and talent. But such external features can be interchangeable. The motivation of the figures is, in each case, similar. They are people (usually men; although women figure prominently in Burla's stories, they are on the receiving end) of great sexual appetite and a nagging ambition which turns out to be insatiable. The author does sometimes don a disguise, using a sub-narrator, or telling a story within a story. But these devices are irrelevant in the characterisation which is of a single hue, directly transferred by the author. And where we have an omniscient narrator, we are still presented with the hero's point of view. This point of view finds it difficult to reflect on itself. The reader is constantly struck by the hero's lack of self-analysis, self-questioning and self-doubt. In Oriental fashion, he accepts the terms of his fate (kismet), even though to the reader it is clear that events have been manipulated by human agency. We also notice that the character does not develop beyond the datum assumed at the outset. Even when things turn out badly, and time remains to effect change, rectification is not permitted by the religious sense of acceptance. Although most of the characters are Jewish, the Islamic context is pervasive, and it shapes events and fortunes of individual and plot. From his earliest work to his latest in the 1960s, Burla's heroes are in the control of external forces – God, religion and social *mores*. However strong the individual impulse to rebel, man is brought to the heel of society, and eventually, often tragically after an attempted breakaway, he submits. This is what happens in *Baal Beamaw (A Substantial Man)*, 1962, where the individualistic hero, Gideon, wants to burst free of the life marked out for him as a gravedigger (his ambition is to be a shepherd). He also aspires to marry a Muslim girl. But opposition from both families imposes disaster.

The Burla story is an old-fashioned moral tale with a dynamic plot and a single hero. Of this type of storyteller Burla is a supreme example. For all his exoticism, he does not constitute an anachronism in modern Hebrew literary life, but has made an invaluable contribution to it.

From a various and rich scene we have made only limited selections, though individual literary characterisation should offer some sense of the range of Palestinian Hebrew literature in the pre-Israeli phase. Although there is not much geography, there is a lot of history. Rarely can so much have happened to so small a nation in so short a time. The variety of provenance, the violence and diversity of events, the range of talent, the extent of the revolutionary ambition have all left their mark on a vital literature, in poetry and prose.

6 IS THERE A FRENCH JEWISH LITERATURE?

In both contemporary and historical terms, French Jewry is of special importance for two reasons. At the moment, French Jewry is by quite a margin the largest in Western Europe, and so numerically the fourth in the world. But beyond that, it is the setting where the theory of political and social emancipation has been tested most sharply. It was in France after the Revolution that the declaration of the 'rights of man' was issued, and that equality was proclaimed for all, regardless of race, religion and status, in respect of these rights. The Jews of France then were invited to assimilate as equal participants into French civilisation, which, needless to say, was considered the most advanced at that time (particularly by the French themselves). The implied question could be drawn out and made explicit. Could Jewry survive and survive creatively in conditions of positive integration into an attractive host culture?

But on examination, the question turns out to be more compounded than the simple formulation would suggest. A theoretical proposition does not necessarily entail implementation. The syllogistic implication of equality for the Jews as men does not compel equal treatment and unblemished integration for them. And the Jewish reaction can be either, on the one hand, defensively negative, seeking absorption and only retreating into a Jewish fortress when necessary, or, on the other, positively espousing a Jewish assertion. In regard to the first sort of reaction, cultural and social assimilation seemed to proceed apace after the Revolution for about a hundred years, on the basis of an egalitarian assumption. This does not mean that French Jewry envisaged the disappearance of itself or of world Jewry. But it could operate confidently within a French context, and take the local situation as a model for the rest. It was from and in France that the first international organisation of Jewry was set up, the 'Alliance Israelite Universelle' of 1860. This was and remains a charitable, social and educational instrument of great dimensions, founded by the well-established French community to succour and support Jewry everywhere. So the concept of world Jewry in concrete, organisational terms originated here, and naturally took on a French character. The programmatic execution seemed to suggest too a successful integration of Frenchness and Jewishness with neither reducing the other. The French model was the ultimate in aspiration, where the fruits of European culture had been distributed through the progressive revolutionary doctrine, as modified by successive legislation. Here the Jew suffered no theoretical disability. It was against this backdrop of assumptions that the shock waves of the Dreyfus affair in the 1890s so stirred the Jews of France, as well as those beyond its borders, who had shared the implicit assumptions of the French lawmakers. If this could happen in France a hundred years after the Revolution, would it ever be possible for Jews to be assimilated? It was the question that Herzl and Nordau posed to suggest a negative answer. Anti-Semitism could survive a century of purveyed culture, theory, goodwill and integration. The totally unjustified condemnation of the General and the supporting anti-Jewish outcry indicated to some a more ambivalent attitude to the Jews than was suggested by the formally logical extension of notional equality. For the Jewish community of the time, it was the formative experience and, even on the sidelines, a note of caution was introduced.

There were Jews in France before the Franks, the Normans and the Burgundians, indeed from the first century onwards. And in Christian France, they shared the fate of Jews in the Christian world generally, sometimes tolerated, sometimes expelled, as in 1306, but always recognisably delimited. 1789 was to change all that, and all barriers henceforth were formally dismantled. How did the Jew in his writing see his own position? Was there a specific Jewish literature either in context or in form, in the things written or in the manner presented? In France the alternatives could be stark, because Jewish affiliation was put as an option. Liberalism at its most liberal allowed the individual Jew to select his attachment and offered the most favourable conditions for assimilation or voluntary membership of the Jewish community. Writing in French of itself implied adoption of French culture and therefore cultural assimilation. But were there invisible strings attached? Did promulgation of the French message imply a total loyalty to some exclusive notion of Frenchness, French history, French religion, perhaps exclusive of Jewish loyalty and Jewish history? The Jewish writer could be just Jewish in a purely subsidiary incidental sense, whilst writing as an individual within a French tradition, shaped by this language, this source of reference and audience. Or he might be aware of another history, another audience, even of another language register. He might also waver between the two, and move from one to the other. Or he might aspire to one and be enveigled by the other.

French Jewish history in modern times has been marked and determined by three great events — the Revolution, the Dreyfus trial and the Nazi occupation and deportations. This is the dialectic of acceptance/rejection. The revolutionary reassessment of the Jewish position was not unconditional, and successive French governments (particularly in Napoleonic times) wanted assurances of exclusive Jewish loyalty to France. The Dreyfus trial indicated continued French suspicion of the Jews, and the intractability of the anomaly. The collapse of the French government in the Second World War, the collaboration with the Nazis and Vichy submission marked the nadir of anti-Jewish practice, as it did elsewhere in Europe. It is in the post-war phase that French Jewry has assumed its central place in European Jewry. The main reason is, of course, negative, i.e. the destruction of European Jewry. The other is the massive influx of North Africans in 1962. In 1971, French Jewry was estimated at 580,000 souls (*Guide Juif de France*), or even 650,000 in 1978 (Bensimon). This puts France well beyond the second West European Community in Britain, and gives a unique voice to Sephardi Jewry in a European framework. There is a synthesis of elements (Neher). Apart from Israel, France is the only Jewish community that has undergone a radical demographic transformation. Jewish writing then will reflect this as it reflects the ambivalence of loyalties, attachment to Jewry and interpretation of its themes and destiny.

There are thse who would deny the existence of Jewish literature in France as a separate category. In an interview conducted on this issue, the critic de Boisdeffre says, 'I would tend to think that up to the war of '39 (and in spite of the Dreyfus Affair), assimilation proceeded apace, that the constituency that you describe as regionalist Jewish, perhaps existed in Alsace, but was otherwise virtually invisible. Emmanuel Berl should be treated as a French writer (by the way as a great writer). And the same with Albert Cohen. It wouldn't occur to me to put them in a special slot' (*L'Arche*, 1979). Here, there is no further analysis of Jewish writing, whether self-aware or objectively such. What he does assert is that France, sociologically, can have no Jewish writing in the sense that exists for example, in New York. In answer to a further question, the critic and historian of the French novel does agree that the French Jewish writer may try to reaffirm the past and express his attachment to it. But he argues that this is not a particularly Jewish trait, and can be discerned along a broad spectrum of view both amongst Jews, and as between Jews and non-Jews. Indeed, he sees assimilation as a virtue from which both parties to the process, the body assimilated and the absorbing body, can gain. 'I see in the literary

French chessboard a Jewish Parisian intelligentsia which has long played a substantial rôle. It goes from Bernard Lazare to Elie Wiesel and through Jules Isaac. And there is in the French University a Liberal Jewish tradition, which is not however fundamentally different from the French University tradition' (ibid). Apart from the fact that there are far more Jews in New York than in Paris which would enable a school of writing to emerge, the critic also holds that France is a far more absorbent nation than the USA which preserves different societies within itself. It would emerge from this analysis that it is France rather than the USA which is a melting pot, and that the latter is more like a salad bowl, with the individual components recognisable, preserving their own separate identities. In such a melting pot, there cannot be a separate or even a distinct Jewish literature.

There is, of course, a different view, expressing itself at its most radical in its perception of a Semitic writing as opposed to Japhetic: 'Japhetic culture makes an abstraction of man, is absorbed by the pursuit of the *thing in itself,* of the object, the absolute, the principle. Its centre of gravity is something very distant, the Copernican system conceived moves towards a sun millions of miles from us' (Rais, *Le Monde Juif,* 1950). In this, the Japhetic conception, the individual person is reduced to nothing but a tiny part of the scheme. Whereas the Jewish view is, continues Rais – as stated in Mishnah *Avot,* where someone who interrupts his learning in order to observe a beautiful, natural phenomenon, is condemned – 'Nature is nothing but God's creation, not admirable for its own sake, but as a witness to God's wisdom . . . This is why, for the Jewish poet, Nature is always granted a significance beyond itself, and is only a metaphorical term, a sign in an alphabetic system of reference. It would never of itself be the centre, never be the end, the centre. The quintessence of the Jewish world is anthropocentrism' (ibid). For the Jew, God is a live being not an abstract concept; the God of the forefathers, not of the philosophers. 'This is the nub of all Jewish culture, nothing is closed off, nothing forbidden, only the accent is other directed – all natural phenomena are considered not in themselves, in principle, in abstract, but as a function of man at the centre. It is for men that God created the world, and it is under this aspect that the Jewish poet views Him, even if he thinks himself an atheist' (ibid). Rais argues that the Jewish writer is basically a different animal, although his situation is complicated by the various degrees of cultural assimilation: 'The most beautiful oak is the one that bears least resemblance to a lime tree and that would be most difficult to mistake for any other species. It would be the most specific oak, the most typical of all; the hybrid, the one of uncertain category is only on the periphery' (*Monde Juif*, 1949). And this is so in literature too. Jewish poetry, when most itself, is utterly different as with Edmond Fleg and André Spire. These 'not only proclaim themselves Jews in their choice of subjects (to the extent that the subject is the result of a deliberate choice with a real poet), but also as regards the interior structure of their works. It is enough for a Jew to be a poet in any language for him to be a Jewish poet. The only necessary condition is sincerity and honesty with himself. It is enough, in sum, to be whatever one is without sacrificing the essential elements of one's personality to the fallacious illusion of assimilationist snobbery' (ibid). With the Bible, non-Jews tend to treat it freely. The Jewish poet, says Rais, is far from the classical, alexandrine form and from prose poetry (the post-Symbolist tendency): 'The Western world has a penchant for the static, for affirmation and construction. The Jew, on the other hand, is a mobile, dialectical element' (ibid).

This separate character has been difficult to describe or even to isolate in prose. Other descriptions of the Jewish novel stress, as did de Boisdeffre, the basic homogeneity of French culture: 'France has the genius of unity, no talent for diversity, no taste for pluralism' (Blot). This view would not deny the Jewish character of a novel, but would primarily locate it in response to a given historical circumstance such as the holocaust, which undermined the French Jew's basic sense of self-identification with his country, or Israel's success in the six day war which suddenly transformed the status of that country (and collective Jewish existence) and so, secondarily, the non-Israeli Jew's status in his own and in others' eyes.

There are then three different views presented as to the character of Jewish writing in France: (1) that there is essentially no such thing except as a regional, local and transient phenomenon. So-called 'Jewish' writing in French writing that can be characterised within the overall Jewish spectrum of French literature; (2) that French Jewish writing certainly exists. It responds in varying degrees of intensity to historical circumstances, and reflects a Jewish sense of insecurity, pride or uncertainty; (3) that there is Jewish writing of a character so specific that it not only has a colour determined by its overt subject matter and response, but which is intrinsic to its very nature and language.

The classic French exposition of Jewish loyalty was made by Edmond Fleg (1872-1964), and more clearly and programmatically in *Pourquoi je suis Juif* than elsewhere. It is the familiar autobiographical outline of a Jew on the fringes of Jewry moving from the periphery to the centre, i.e. to an unqualified stance of adherence to and faith in Jewry's future. As the title indicates (it is one of a series of statements 'why I am'), the work is constituted as a credo, offering the principal features and structure of his life, history and being. Written both in the form of an autobiography and statement to his son (as yet unborn) for the future, it presents both his past attitudes and his present expectations. He tries to tie the present conditon of Judaism and Jewry to their history. Will they survive? Or, to put it another way, will there still be Jews in 1960? 'I think so. They survived the Pharoahs, Nebuchadnezzar, Constantine, Mohammed, the Inquisition and assimilation. They will also survive the car.' Judaism may have seemed to be precarious in the 1920s, he says, but it has seemed so very often before, has faced and survived many conditions and challenges. Most recently, it managed to persist in the face of the persuasive lure of modern Europe. Characteristic of the new culture is technology, which offers a challenge of a different, impersonal, secular character. For whatever reason and in whatever guise, and although we may be unable to forcast how, it will persist, says Fleg in his statement of faith, into and beyond the technological era. It can even be resurrected. Judaism can die and be reborn, as happened in respect of the author himself.

He proceeds then to his autobiographical sketch to illustrate this precise point. He describes the Judaism of his youth, Jewish life as he knew it, as 'a mixture of all sorts of life actions, conducted though in so simple a manner that I didn't think of this as Judaism'. He apparently did not understand what was going on, nor was the matter satisfactorily explained to him. Which indicates that the tie was emotional rather than rational. His link with Judaism was made fast by the joy associated with it, not by a convincing presentation of ordered argument for its preservation. And it was this, in later years, that must have served as the bedrock for its reinstatement. The Passover, for example: 'Of all that it was supposed to say I was ignorant; I asked neither others nor myself. I knew only one thing; that my parents' face held, at these moments, a radiance of joy and serenity that I have only observed since on the portraits of the greatest saints.' The child had clear religious yearnings, but his Jewish attachment was to be disturbed later by the ritualistic inconsistency of his parents and the ignorance of his teachers. He was indeed tempted by Christianity in his search for total faith. He wrote then: 'God, put Your light into me, show me if You exist.' With Fleg, the move from Geneva to Paris was decisive; it was a move from youth to adulthood: 'In Geneva, where I was born, the clans were totally separated; I had lived nothing other than a Jewish life. Our ghetto was no longer locked in by chains; but it remained a ghetto.' And it was in Paris that he seemed to lose his religious appetite, becoming a humanist in the fashion of Comte and then a fashionable aesthete, raising Art to the level of a religion. Both the relativistic notion of society and the evaluation of Art replaced Judaism, which then assumed a confining and abject posture.

And then along came the Dreyfus affair in 1894. The camps divided, and there peeped through a subliminal loyalty. Why otherwise should this affair have mattered so much? Judaism seemed to be on its deathbed, even perceptible in the growing assimilationist tendency of his family: 'In the patriarchal set up, Israel was already so sick, that if it was going to die everywhere, as it had died in me, there was nothing to do but let it.' But the Dreyfus affair tested the thesis, and it aroused not just general human solidarity, but a specifically Jewish sense. It had made the 'Jewish question' live for him, although it was also thus tragic. Was he then a Zionist, one of the followers of Herzl, himself impelled to adopt this radical solution by observing and reporting that same affair? Yes, indeed, he had become a Zionist. But he remained too very French. A new point in his development: 'Therefore, then, abandoning the egoism of the dilettante, I started looking in the depths of myself for a tradition, and found it . . . the French tradition mixed with the Jewish.' Zionism would be exciting, particularly for the three million [quite an estimate!] who would live in Israel: 'But for the twelve million who will stay dispersed round the world, for all those, and for myself, the tragic question remains What is Judaism? What must a Jew do? How is one a Jew? Why be a Jew?' So he decided to take off some years to study Judaism. He looked for proof of God, and found it in the persistent existence of the Jewish people. He says in summary: 'I am Jewish, because born of Israel and having lost it, I have felt its revival in me, more alive than myself.' He would transmit that sense to his son as 'all the fathers' have transmitted it to him and, more importantly, through him, through the blood. And this blood will continue to flow, despite any defections, 'to the last days'. This passion moves Fleg here, in his work and his long life in general, and in his poems on Jewish themes as collected in the volume *Écoute, Israël: Et tu aimeras L'Eternel*, whose title is the beginning of the central prayer of the Jewish faith, the Shema. These poems are often set in the past. But they concern the future too, the Jewish future in the forms of Messianic expectation.

Ideologically, the poet André Spire (1868-1966) made a similar turn to

Fleg. Like Fleg he 'discovered' Judaism, and was thus born again. In his *Poèmes Juifs,* he narrows this discovery down further: 'Had I refound faith? Not at all. But (I had found) my ancestors, my race, the Judaism of my early youth. I once again became Jewish with a capital J.' Like Fleg, he also juxtaposed Frenchness and Jewishness to combine the two, because he adds there: 'A French poet and a Jewish poet as well.' He struggles with the definition of Jewish poet, a title he had been unambiguously awarded, not only by himself, but even by such as G. Sorel in 1908, who wrote: 'Here is the Jewish soul across time. Spire from this moment on has marked out his place amongst those who live, fight, die for the raising of Jewish dignity.' Spire writes in his 1919 introduction: 'Our poems are not Jewish by subject, but by sentiment.' Of course, if selection of subject were to determine the Jewish nature of a work, then anyone could opt for this category. But Spire declares an empathy:

'You ask me why I like these pariahs
The sole proletariat in which I can hope.'

For Spire, Judaism is not an abstract category, but a current reality expressed through Jewish life and history. The Jewish story is suffering past and present, and its obsession is with a God who has betrayed His people. The Torah, Law, practice, commandment, faith, have ears 'only for the tears which fall from the four corners of the universe', not for pleasure or joy. The Jews remain

'a people without rights, a people without land:
A nation tortured by all the nations'.

He invites them to dream of the 'destroyed temple' and declare undying faith in the treacherous God. That is Israel's constant strength. This is his Jewish world, so different from the French world (that of his culture and language):

'Come to defend me
Against the dry reason of this happy land.'

He has to select from the two warring elements in his necessary makeup. But he finds the smooth, quintessential Frenchness cloying.

What does Israel want? In his poem 'Assimilation', he quotes Renan:

'Israel aspires to two contradictory things,
to be like the whole world and to be apart.'

This poem comments on the irony of the Jew as *nearly* Christian, whose nose is almost straight (and, after all, some Christians have a crooked nose). But there is still a qualitative distinction. They are happy,

'but you, what are you doing in your corner, awkward and sad,
Full of pity, full of scorn?'

What the Jew should do is to be true to himself and 'chase' his ancient soul which has come here (i,e, to France) to look for 'you'. It is here that the French/Jewish struggle takes place within the individual. The Jew cannot be, or, at least, is not at ease within the Christian environment, in a Christian home. The concerns of the two are so different. The Christian in France worries about his tea, his game of bridge, his theatres. He is concerned in sum, he says to him 'for your dear tranquillity'. That is French civilisation, and in this respect the Christian has reason to be wary of the Jew who is so different:

'You are right, as between us two,
To fear somewhat, comrade!
For they only live in a fever
My two ancient protectors:
My unease, my sadness.'

The contrast is grasped as that between the 'present' and the 'eternal' in his poem 'Le Messie':

'Art, if I were to accept you, my life would be charming.
My days would pass lightly, pleasantly, gracefully.
I would hold and possess the transient Present.
— But would my heart, content still live
If you tore from it its splendid dream:
Eternal tomorrow that marches ahead?'

But it is not solely the morrow that marches into view of Spire's poems. He calls to sing 'the sublime today' through the person of Music. Israel will be resurrected and proud, as in the poem 'Exode' which ends:

'And amongst the honey of your bees,
The milk of your ewes, the grape of your vines,
You will see stand erect, revived and young
Your pride, Israel.'

Spire's poems after 1918 became increasingly Zionistic. They see the present Jewish condition as being amenable to political amelioration in the renewed sense of nationhood. Now is the moment to be exploited. In his poem 'A la Nation Juive', he writes:

'You are still worthy to live.
The land of your fathers will be given to you
. . . But you hesitate.
You have to break so many chains:
Apprehensively, you wonder:
Is this the end of the exile? Is it the beginning?'

In these poems by Spire, the Jews are sometimes the theme, but always the inspiration. Like the other French Jewish authors, those committed to both these categories, Spire feels drawn between the two centres, and is forced to observe and contrast. The world of the immediate, of the pleasant, is attractive but essentially frivolous. The other world is demanding, but real and eternal. In a political sense, the two time scales can be united. Emergency demands urgency, and the Jews can transmute their permanent destiny into present policy.

As noted above, one of the most interesting features of the French scene is the voice given to Sephardi Jewry, that Jewry from a Muslim rather than a Christian environment. Identity can only be discovered and then defined in relation to something different. The Jews in France from North Africa have, by virtue of their situation, been aware of three groupings, however, shaded and modified — African Muslim, French Christian and Jewish. Albert Memmi (b. 1920), originally from Tunis, is not only interesting because of his circumstances, but in the way that he has attempted through these circumstances to cast light on his situation and identity, and to investigate the meaning of his Jewishness against a backdrop not intimately familiar to the Western world. His earliest and most lasting concern is with his own identity: 'I was descended from a Berber tribe not recognised by the Berbers, because I was a Jew and non-Muslim, a city and not a mountain dweller . . . Indigenous in a country of colonisation, Jewish in an anti-semitic environment, African in a world where Europe was triumphant' *(Portrait d'un Juif)*. He was a puzzle, to others and indeed to himself too, which had to be investigated. He was universally not accepted, as a sympathiser with the colonised although himself a non-Muslim, as a Jew although non-European, as a bourgeois, as a deracinated North-African. He discovers that Oriental Jews have not been heard much in intellectual, Occidental circles. Those same circles which have little precise information about Islam and its contemporary condition, but are possessed either by ravaging colonial ambitions or romantically hazy notions. As a spokesman of this hybrid condition, Memmi presents not only his Judaism, but also his understanding of Islam. The Jewish condition that he isolates he terms 'Judeity', in parallel to 'Negreity' i.e. negritude. This Judeity is the recognition of the fact of being a Jew, as distinct from Judaism − a religion − or Jewry, which is the neutral term for the body of Jews as a collective, regardless of self-identification. It would apply to those who feel that they, by being Jewish and as Jews, would nurture this character in some way.

Memmi's book *Juifs et Arabes* presses the point that, on the one hand, Oriental Jews in Israel are underrepresented, and, on the other, that the situation of the Jews in Muslim countries is little known. The 'Jewish question' has been perceived in the West as one peculiar and limited to Christian culture, and Zionism too has been thought of as a Western European phenomenon. But Arab lands had and still have their Jewish ghettos too, and 'who could visit them without shock?' Contradicting the impression fostered that any such bad relations as do exist originate with Zionism, Zionism, in fact, flourished as an earlier by-product of the oppression of Jews in these places. It is true that the Arabs were colonised by Europe. But the Jews in Arab lands suffered a double colonisation as Natives, and then as non-Arabs. Memmi does not deny the right of Palestinians to determine their fate as a nation, but, he says, there are two rights: 'Both of us have and still remain victims of human history; our two stories are remarkably parallel.' What tragically but inevitably took place between Israel and the Arab world was an exchange of populations. In brief, the Oriental Jew shares the 'common Jewish condition'. What then of the 'Judéité' that he formulated? 'Judeity is not only the manner of being, more or less transient, on the part of the subject. Being Jewish is a condition imposed on each Jew, largely from the outside; it is mainly then the result of relations between Jews and non-Jews.' This may sound like Sartre's negative definition of a Jew. But for Sartre 'a Jew is a person considered as such by others. This strikes me as insufficient. A Jew, for me, above all, someone *treated* as such by others, and capable of being treated still worse.' Judeity has to have reality in live transaction. And as for the liberal assumption that the Jew could and should assimilate into the general culture, Memmi holds that this general culture, even if apparently secularised, is fundamentally religious, thus cutting off Jewish experience from any other: 'In brief, to be Jewish is not to participate fully in the dominant culture, not to attend the same temple as his co-citizens, not to live the same collective rhythms, not always to react with the same sensibility, with all the consequences thereby implied.'

The author sums up what is, for him, to be a Jew, under three headings: (1) to have an awareness of so being; (2) that there be an objective condition (i.e. that the subject is actually Jewish, and is treated as such by others); (3) to belong to a certain culture. The Jew indubitably is. He exists. But he is also oppressed. And the Jews are oppressed not solely in a particular respect, but in all collective dimensions. In other words, we must admit that they are oppressed as a people: 'Consequently, oppressed as a people, Jews will not be genuinely liberated, except as a people. Today, liberation of peoples has a national character.' Zionism is the logical outcome of his position, a Zionism which naturally does not infringe any positive social or egalitarian principle, but rather confirms them. After all, what is the alternative? To be an Arab Jew? 'Objectively, as they say, there are no Jewish communities in any Arab country: and you will not find a single Arab Jew who would be prepared to return to his country of birth.' And this for the reason stated: the Jewish experience in the Arab world has been as negative as in the Christian world. It has been the State of Israel's simple but sublime function to put an end to Jewish oppression —past, present and potential. The Jew colonised can become Israel liberated, without any necessarily detrimental effects on other groups which seek their own liberation. Memmi has moved from a realisation of the anomalous position of the Jew under Islam to a recognition of the Jew's nationhood, and thus to the vehicle for the expression of this nationhood in Zionism and contemporary Israel.

No recent novel by any French Jewish writer has made a greater impact than *Le Dernier des Justes (The Last of the Just)* by André Schwarz-Bart (b. 1928). It is a reflection not only on the holocaust but on the course of Jewish fate, through history and mythical statement. But the proposition of the book is ambivalent. That there have been thirty-six (lamed-vav) just men in each generation, often unknown to others and sometimes even to themselves, has been recounted from the time of the Talmud. But this novel both speculates on the function of the just man (tzadik), and suggests that this particular line of the just, the Levys, has now come to an end. A just man is born to martyrdom in the popular and the literal sense, to suffer and to bear witness. This particular line of the Levys is traced to York, 1185. Of course, there had been martyrdoms before, all throughout Europe, but the martyrdom of Yom Tov Lévy 'was raised beyond communal tragedy to become legend'. The legend is that 'the world is based on thirty-six just men, the lamed-vav, not distinguished in any way from ordinary mortals, sometimes unknown to themselves'. They are necessary 'because the lamed-vavs are the intensified heart of the world, and all our sorrows are poured into them, as into a receptacle'. They are like other people, only more so, and they stand for collective Jewish experience. They are tragic cases, and most tragic of all are those who do not know what they really are.

The Levys are present at the expulsions from various European countries — England, France, Spain, etc. and suffer in the pogroms. In nineteenth-century Poland, Mordecai Levy, grandfather of the 'last just', Ernie, is asked why the lamed-vav has to suffer so. The answer is that he 'takes our suffering upon himself . . . and he raises it to heaven, and sets it at the feet of the Lord who forgives. Which is why the world goes on . . . in spite of all our sins.' He does not have to work a miracle, because he is a miracle. Then the next generation (Benjamin) moves to Warsaw. And then on to Berlin, where something new happens; Benjamin ceases to believe in the legend, indeed does not want to believe in it. Benjamin's son Ernie in Hitler's Germany declares: 'God is not here. He's forgotten us.' When Ernie hears the legend, he also learns that the suffering of the lamed-vav will not change anything. The just men may 'glow', but nothing happens. Mordecai thinks that suffering is only of service to glorify the Name, but Ernie, now enlisted in France 1938, 'felt the same old amazement that there was no rhyme or reason to the universe'. This is what he consciously avers, and he may say it. But his life speaks otherwise. Safely out of danger in Marseilles, he chooses to return to occupied Paris, goes back 'into the flames'. But amazingly, in secular terms, he did not join the resistance groups, because 'for him it would have been a luxurious death. He had no wish to singularise himself, or detach himself from the humble processions of the Jewish people.' He may have ceased to believe, but he is acting as a lamed-vav, representing the Jews, containing their suffering playing out the martyr's role. This is what Jesus did in Ernie's view. He presents himself to Drancy, the Paris concentration camp, before being called. With this, he has entered 'the last circle of the Levys' hell'. And he moves further into it, in Auschwitz, entering what has now become the 'kingdom of Israel'.

The Last of the Just is a searing, poetic text, resonant in implication. The legend is ancient, but the suggestion of the novel's title is modern. We are in a post-religious universe, but also in a post-holocaust universe. Not only has the world been stripped of God. It has also been stripped of the residual moral sense that would make the silent martyrdom of the thirty-six meaningful. This implication is not made explicit in the novel, but the chant of the names of the death camps puts an end to more than the novel itself. Mordecai's stated belief that suffering must glorify the Name in order to be meaningful, can now be tested. Is the holocaust the sort of traditional martyrdom familiar to us from the Middle Ages? Is this martyrdom a voluntary God-giving witness, and is there anyone to attend the witness? These are the questions raised by the book in its tantalising title, in the rapid degeneration of the Levys' belief in their own mission, and in the sense of the legend. The world has changed for ever, and in this new world, there is no place for the 'just man'.

A very different view of a past Jewish world in a new European context is presented to us in *Le Livre de ma Mère* by Albert Cohen (b. 1895), a moving rhapsody on the author's now dead mother. That he can devote such a passionate book to her sounds incestuous. Clearly, his mother represents his youth, his past, an old world. And her death is for him the death of his childhood. 'To mourn your mother is to mourn your youth.' With her death 'my death approaches'. Her death is a reminder to him of his mortality. It also fills him with guilt, as he feels that he had not appreciated her sufficiently. Perhaps also that he had been away from her, at the time of her demise, in London. Now they are both condemned to loneliness: 'All over, all over, no more mother, never. We are both really alone, you in the ground, me in my room. I, somewhat dead amongst the living, your a bit alive amongst the dead.'

This is also a sort of autobiography, but an obsessive one devoted to this one subject. His father is hardly mentioned, except to remark in passing that he is usually out at work. When the author moves to Geneva from his home town of Marseilles at the age of eighteen, his mother's isolation (her marriage was one of convenience) seems total. The highlights of her life are her annual visits to him in Geneva. Otherwise, she is busy writing to him, worrying about him, and taking pride in his literary and general success. Her obsession with him must have been as complete as his with her. But his concern follows her death. She also has represented the old world of Judaism, dead for him. In her foreignness (originally they are from Corfu) and in her superstition, she is clearly that bit Jewish. She wants him to go to synagogue even if he is an atheist, and to observe other religious ceremonies too, as some protection against the evil eye. This expression of her origin estranges her from her French environment, and she is conscious that her son has soared beyond his humble origins. Now that she is dead, he is consumed by guilt. As he did not love her sufficiently, and was not as considerate of her as he should have been, he now seeks to make some notional compensation. He had hardly written to her, so he now rebukes himself: 'You did not want to write ten words, so now write forty thousand.' Her love for him, on the other hand, knew no bounds, although he had done little to merit it: 'My mother's love had no compare. She lost all judgement as far as her son was concerned. She accepted all of me, possessed by a divine spirit which sensed the loved one, the poor loved one, so little divine.' He can never be loved like that again, unconditionally. His daughter may love him now, but she will naturally move on and away. His mother had a genius for love as others may have a genius for art. Now he is totally desolate without her: 'I am a fruit without a tree, a chick without a hen, a cub alone in the desert, and I am cold. I want to be Mama's little boy. Ridiculous to talk like this at my age? But then, that's the way it is.'

An exercise in self-exposure, this book also remarks the inevitability of the situation. Those alive are condemned to live and to enjoy life, so offending against the dead. But, of course, they too will, in turn become dead, and be offended against. At least, dead, she is no longer Jewish: 'Eyes of living Jews are always afraid. That is our speciality, misfortune.' He wants to believe in life eternal after death when he can meet his mother again. But for that he requires convincing support for such a faith. Such support is presumably not forthcoming.

This very partial summary of aspects of modern Jewish writing in France indicates some ways in which the Jewish theme is manifest. There are others too. Recent history has been noticeably marked and marred by the Jewish experience. Maurice Bessy's novel *Car c'est Dieu qu'on Enterre* (a quotation from a Pasternak poem) tells of a hundred Jewish women being deported for extermination. It is God that is being buried now, suggests the title, not just these women. And there are other memorials to this dreadful and, for some of the authors, spiritually conclusive history, like Manès Sperber's *Plus Profond que L'Abîme*. Also that excellent example of modern Jewish picaresque, Arnold Mandel's *Tikoun*. Israel is grasped by many of the authors as having a special fate and atmosphere, difficult to isolate because it is so mingled with their own French perception and their ordinary life. But it is still in some respects distinct. For Memmi, there is the category of 'Judéité', the manner of living that cannot be totally contained by either 'Judaism' (the religion) or 'Judaicité' (the people, Jewry). For Schwarz-Bart there is a special fate, although that might have come to an end with the passing of the 'last of the just'. For Spire, there is a sense of the eternal contrasted with the French feeling for the immediate. For Fleg, there is a particular instinct which has carved the Jew out another place, and which can surface at times of testing crisis. These are aspects of a Jewish view of the world and of itself within a French context.

7 FROM THE PERIPHERY TO THE CENTRE IN AMERICA

America, by the end of World War I, had become the greatest Jewish centre in the world, both in number and influence. Immigrants continued to stream in through to the mid-1920s, and so their concern initially was to establish themselves and to assimilate successfully and tidily into the new environment. They had to find homes and jobs, to learn the language and to be acceptable as American citizens. In the literature of American Jews we find a predominant preoccupation with ethnic identity and assimilation. The physical fact of being Jewish raised the question of ethnic loyalty, religion as a determinant of status, the possibility of intermarriage, the meaning of Americanism. American Jewish fiction of the pre-second war period amply illustrates this focus in a variety of guises and talents.

But then the immigration was absorbed, the ghettos (to a large extent) dispersed, the communities Americanised. By the 1940s, a substantial native-born generation considered itself as much part of the national fabric as any other element, religious or ethnic. To be an American Jew became increasingly one of the ways of being an American. Ethnical marginality was no longer the primary concern, except in the specific case of the European immigration in the wake of the holocaust. This did not mean that there was no longer a characteristically Jewish literature but its form of expression changed. The Jew could not easily see himself as an immigrant if he was of local provenance and an English-speaking American national. He was already, on the whole, commercially successful, socially established if not totally integrated, and did not have another mother country to look back to nostalgically or to summon as a measure. He was not an outsider in that he belonged to a Jewry of another time, another place. The immediate difficulty of acclimatisation had been overcome.

It might be thought that in the process of acculturation and assimilation there would be no more place to speak of a distinctive Jewish voice on the American scene. But, it is by the 1940s, and certainly in the decades following, that the Jewish voice is not only heard but increasingly accepted as the norm. Jewish terminology, except in certain instances of specialist exposition, is no longer explained to the reader. Yiddish has entered the American language, and the Jewish type with the implications of his cultural, social and historical background is understood as part of the scene. Bellow does not have to translate to the extent that Cahan did. And the Jew is not seen on the fringes of society, trying to edge his way in. In many ways, he exemplifies that society. And Jewish literature is peculiarly American literature. In William Styron's novel, *Sophie's Choice*, set in the immediate post-war period, a leading character, Nathan Landau, predicts a Jewish literary fashion as emerging predominant amongst the various regional or ethnic genres. He claims that the first indication of this is the publication of Saul Bellow's *Dangling Man* in 1944.

With the removal of the Jew from the periphery to the centre, and his portrayal without his most distinguishing features in terms of language, religious belief, ethnic affiliations and social ties, the definition of Jewish literature becomes once more problematic. The problem is indeed part of the definition. The writers to be discussed here will see the Jew, or the self or the 'person' in many different ways. The character in a novel, or the narrator, or the writer behind, may not be in any obvious sense Jewish, and the creator might strenuously resist such a possibly restrictive label. But there are nevertheless quite unmistakable Jewish features, even when veiled. The Jew may appear in different disguise in Trilling's novel, in the guise of the constant and unwilling victim in the stories of Malamud, as restless suburbanite in Bellow, as irremediably neurotic in Philip Roth. These writers may all see themselves as generally American rather than specifically Jewish. Nevertheless, they can be better understood within a Jewish context, which might be enlightening rather than restrictive, bringing with it another historical dimension echoing with past experiences. But now this is middle-of-the-road American literature rather than specialist ethnic material, as borne out by both its pervasiveness throughout American life and culture, and by its commercial success.

Lionel Trilling (1905-75) wrote one novel, *The Middle of the Journey*, the work of a highly talented literary critic. In this, John Laskell, recuperating from a crippling case of scarlet fever, lives through his recent past and an involvement with one Gifford Maxim, one-time Communist Party activist, and in the present, with his liberal hosts, the Crooms. The book is concerned with the attitudes of the Crooms to Maxim's defection and to Laskell's past illness. The assumptions of the Crooms, their friends and associates, and of the main character, Laskell, are progressive. Although they were not Party members, nor even officially Fellow Travellers, they were and remain broadly sympathetic to Party aims, and they regard Maxim's defection as unforgivable betrayal. Maxim had been the one to influence and involve them, so his defection undermines the ground of their past activities and their current stance. Perhaps the Crooms simply cannot face negativity, or even the plain reality of life like the Moscow trials, Laskell's illness and the fact of death. The novel, set in the late 1930s, describes the current fashionable mentality: 'People of liberal mind understood that the belief in Moscow's domination of the Party in America had been created by the reactionary Press, and they laughed at it.' The puzzle for the contemporary reader is that an educated person of goodwill could latch on to such a nasty ideology. But, in Maxim's interpretation, they were of the 'disaffected portion of the middle class'. These are the unaffiliated, rootless, deracinated and, of course, in the contemporary context, disproportionately Jewish.

Appropriately, in the work of Forster's admirer, Trilling's novel abounds in moral commentary on the characters' actions, and in melodramatic denouement. The child of the admired factotum, Duck, dies after he has hit her. Who is responsible? Was Laskell party to that event, as Maxim, once professional killer, might like? The moralist needs companionship in guilt. He says: ' "I will get out of the system by admitting my guilt".' Everyone is responsible for the consequences of his actions, he asserts. But, unlike Communism, his new faith, Christianity, admits an element of mercy. Is his categorisation correct? Is his a leader's morality, assigning and accepting responsibility, and the Crooms' a mass ethic, shelving responsibility? And where does Laskell stand in all this? He has accepted the implied, prevalent attitude, liberal although not totally committed to the agency of change. And he too was horrified at Maxim's turnabout.

It is Laskell who is at the heart of the book and its mystery. He, like so many of the other characters, seems to be unrooted in any convincing social reality. He is ethnically neutered and religiously humanistic. As for the gullibility, it could bear out the thesis that a sceptic does not believe in nothing. Rather, he is capable of believing in anything. Even such an unlikely candidate as Soviet Communism makes a totalitarian appeal. The Jew's experience in America has led him, amongst other things, to Communism, as we have seen in other contexts. But this is a novel not grounded in ethnic or specific experience, so both the predilections and tendencies of the characters and the plot development seem eccentric and arbitrary. Fiedler has it that Trilling tried to write 'the story of the allure of Communism and the disillusion with it'. A very large and important subject. But a novel requires treatment different from a learned discourse and must be clothed in a flesh and blood social and human reality. A great part of this allure, and probably the backdrop to the related events, applied largely to the Jews. Here, the context has been generalised into unrecognisable Americanism, and so the novel has lost a great deal of its realisable potential. Forster has been translated into another environment, but not one of sufficient concreteness for all the appealing guise that Trilling's talent lends it.

Saul Bellow (b. 1915) is a virtuoso writer, most distinguished as technical innovator and in range of language amongst the plethora of Jewish fictionists. His *Dangling Man* sets the tone for his work and presents the hero that will appear regularly in his work. In the course of a writing career extending over forty years thus far this hero has got older, but he always evinces similar features. Each novel is built very much round a particular individual, trying to locate himself within and to establish his character for the world outside. Bellow's first novel is written in the form of a journal so it can indulge the luxury of introspection. And this introspection is a major component of a Bellow story, voicing its opposition to the tradition of gentlemanly restraint. The author gives full vent to feeling, although this is moderated by flashbacks. Excessive self-indulgence too is modified by intervention of other voices. A supple, confessional prose highlights the moods of the diarist, hovering between expectancy (he is awaiting his call-up, and has meanwhile given up employment) and hopelessness at his condition of parasitism. The dangling man is precisely marginal, not fulfilling a useful function in society. Although we hear Joseph moody, bitter, resentful, we can also get a glimpse of Joseph as seen by others and in contrast to a livelier, healthier Joseph of a year back. But his peculiar and very distressing situation does enable him to investigate himself by entering an extreme situation. And he will move into another extreme, as he prepares to join in the war effort: 'To be pushed upon oneself entirely, put the very facts of simple existence in doubt. Perhaps the war could teach me by violence what I had been unable to learn during those months in the room.' Here is the individual first thrown on to his own resources, and then cast into the cell of restriction. Freedom and its opposite may locate the individual: 'Long live regimentation', he concludes.

So many external biographical aspects of Bellow's heroes recur in successive stories. The family relationships echo one another. The large-boned hero, emotional and unstable, with his succession of wives, his rich brother, his dominating, successful father. *Herzog* is about a middle-aged man in crisis, declaring at the outset: 'If I am out of my mind, it's all right with me.' Here, Herzog is at the centre of the novel, manipulating the emotions of everybody else through an endless stream of letters, mostly unsent. He writes to all and sundry, to friends, acquaintance, other scholars, great figures of history, and to God. He is at present going through divorce for a second time and both recalls other relationships and begins to suggest preparations for a third more stable union. He has thus been hitherto unable to establish permanence and focus in his personal life and in his scholarship. The reader though can testify to the dynamism of his relationships and to the brilliance of his scholastic and literary achievements as summarised. But at this stage of life, Herzog is looking for something more, encapsulated in the notion of quiet. The turbulent individual must come to terms with himself and his world. For Herzog this supreme plateau is a condition of not writing letters: 'Nothing. Not a single word,' as the novel concludes.

The Bellow novel does typically work towards a resolution. Intellectual and emotional complexity strive for direction through the choppy seas of distraction. *Herzog* is Bellow's detailed investigation of this state of mind. His scholarship links up with his life. He has studied the connections between Romanticism and Christianity, and he sees himself as living in a post-Christian, post-humanist context of nothingness. Herzog, he says, is part of 'a collective project, himself participating, to destroy his vanity and his pretensions to a personal life, so that he might disintegrate and suffer and hate, like so many others, not on anything so distinguished as a cross, but down in the mire of post-Renaissance, post-humanistic, post-Cartesian dissolution, next door to the Void'. This is the essence of contemporary man as nihilist, believing in nothing, unable (in his case) to return to the comfortable envelopment of the old Jewish heim, beyond the ecstasies and optimisms that flourish in history which he has investigated. As for life around him, even if he is invited to participate in a life-affirming exercise, as by his marvellous new girlfriend Ramona, he cannot accept the invitation. He must destroy the ground of any apparently solid existence. Anything solid would be illusory. Herzog, the middle-aged man, must slay the dragon of illusion, in order to locate the nugget of genuine truth: 'my suffering, if I may speak of it, has often been a more extended form of life, a striving for true wakefulness as an antidote to illusion'. He carries his own self-destruct: 'But some people are at war with the best things of life and pervert them into fantasies and dreams.' His story is 'how I rose from humble origins to complete disaster'.

The resolution that Herzog seems to establish at the end of his novel may be, in his terms, false or temporary. His turbulence is circular, and he must halt in his tracks if he cannot advance. *Mr Sammler's Planet* takes the story of stage further. The hero here, Mr Sammler, is in his seventies. So he has passed beyond the strife, the ambition and the achievement, and can settle back to review both what he has done and the state of the world that he now finds. His 'planet' is far from where he now lives, in New York, vandalised, uncivilised, crime-ridden. He is Polish in origin, and his planet is Europe, where he enunciated a code of behaviour and ethics. Much of the point of the novel is in the contrast drawn between the debased vitality of the city and Mr Sammler's own planet. Youth has 'real' sexual potency. He is invited to deliver a lecture at Columbia University on the England that he knew between the wars. He has drawn his mature idealism from that period and from the figures of literary London – the Bloomsbury group and, more particularly, H. G. Wells. They had offered a sense of optimism, the vision of a future for civilisation in a post-religious world. But that vision had collapsed in the holocaust soon to follow. Present-day New York bears the scars of the destruction rather than of the hope, and Mr Sammler has no contemporary relevance. In the course of his lecture, he is interrupted by a raucous student, who calls out to the youthful audience that they should not listen to him: ' "his balls are dry" '. Then a Negro pickpocket, whom he has spotted in operation, shows him his massive sexual organ. That in itself, is the implication, should suffice to inspire respect and terror in New York today. So Sammler can only see himself through the eyes of others as 'a vestige, a visiting consciousness which happened to reside in a West Side bedroom'.

Sammler's vestigial character is represented by the mode of his survival. He was due to be shot in a mass grave dug by the victims themselves in wartime Poland. His improbable escape emphasises his lack of identification with the new world. And he is now merely a symbol: 'Mr Sammler had a symbolic character. He, personally, was a symbol. His friends and family had made him a judge and a priest. And of what was he a symbol? He didn't even know. Was it because he had survived? He hadn't even done that, since so much of the earlier person had disappeared. It wasn't surviving, it was only lasting.' Wells's world has not survived. He had believed in 'scientific humanism, faith in an emancipated future, in active benevolence, in reason, in civilisation. Not popular ideas at the moment.' A genuine humanism is expressed by his relative, Dr Elya Gruner, his benefactor, progenitor of the sexually experimental Angela and a crazy son, both of whom want his money.

But Gruner has a very precarious existence, and he is on the point of death throughout the novel. The novel's climax comes with his actual death and with Sammler's appreciation of him as one who has successfully met 'the terms of his contract'. That is what it means to be truly human. We all know the terms of our own contract, and we must try to meet them. Bellow's novel attempts to distill the essence of human struggle. It is a diary of the individual's effort to find himself, through his needs and failures, and to resign himself to his true nature.

Both the international experience and European thought had influenced American literature in the direction of Existentialism, i.e. a perception of man through extreme situations. Man creates himself in a situation; that is what existing means. And no experience is more extreme and ultimate than that of death. As death is beyond experience, it is through the shadows of death, the knowledge of death to come, that man can find his existential nature. No-one has been more assiduous in the cultivation of existential man in literature than Norman Mailer (b. 1923). The tone is set for him with the appropriate subject matter of his first novel, *The Naked and the Dead:* 'All over the ship, all through the convoy, there was a knowledge that in a few hours some of them were going to be dead.' In the Mailer scheme, nothing can refine and define the consciousness more than death.

Increasingly over the years, Mailer has turned from fiction to journalism. In order to find the hero at the edge of experience, he has little need to invent situations. He can instead join in mass marches over troubled and significant issues, or write about criminals and great projects. And the hero in his opus is none other than the author himself. In his later work Mailer even sometimes inserts himself in the narrative as a character 'M'. Just as fiction has tended to description of fact in his work, so fact has moved to fiction. Mailer as 'M' is a projected hero, a Hemingway-style ideal, bestriding the edge of the world like an existential colossus. He cannot hold the middle ground as average mortals might have to. He must move to one pole or another: 'Between the saint and the debauchee, no middle ground seemed tenable for his appetites' *(Advertisements for Myself)*. And the hero has to keep investigating himself, as each answer suggests new questions. Ethical judgement of the dynamic human is constantly being made and revised. Self-discovery too cannot be a completed step, but a process in progress. He, his own hero, must be tested. For Hemingway, whose work he admires so, the test could be in war or in bullfighting, experiences exacting courage, devotion, strength and nerve. For Mailer other tamer and more urban, but, in any case, equivalent tests could be devised. He became a public figure and speaker: 'The pleasure of speaking in public was the sensibility it offered: with every phrase one was better or worse, close or less close to the existential promise of truth' *(The Armies of the Night)*. And the type that most merits his admiration is the one open to new experience and challenge, quicksilver. In an essay entitled 'The White Negro' *(Advertisements for Myself)* he spells out the characteristics of the hipster, the man who knows that his fate is to live with death. The Negro is more capable than the white man of fitting into the category, because he, of his nature and the nature of white society, lives in constant danger. So he is attractive to our generation. Danger constantly faces the Negro, so the Negro is contemporary man at his most typical, although also *in extremis*. Life, for all its ugliness, is actually exciting because it poses extreme alternatives. Successful modern man is he who is aware of the nature of society and can cope with it. That is to be, like the Negro, hip: 'Hip is the sophistication of the wise primitive in a giant jungle.' And of our era in general: 'No matter what its horrors the twentieth century is a vastly exciting century for its tendency is to reduce all of life to its ultimate alternatives.'

Mailer as a fictionist is rather less convincing than Mailer the public figure and journalist, hero in his own copy. Like Trilling, he tried to deal with the American experience of Communism in an early novel, *Barbary Shore*. But as in Trilling's *The Middle of the Journey,* the social groundwork of Mailer's novel is unconvincing, and the plot even more unlikely. The narrator, Mikey Lovett, has lost his memory. He may be a war veteran, but he cannot, in the early stages of the narrative, reconstruct his past. He takes a room from a radical playwright in a dilapidated house, and the substance of the novel is the rather unlikely interaction between Lovett and the other tenants, McLeod and Hollingsworth. He is asked by his landlady, a potential mistress as he sees her, to spy on McLeod, who turns out to be not only an old radical but also her husband. In any case, he is investigated by Hollingsworth whose precise function is never clarified (perhaps an American government agent?). The narrator suddenly and inexplicably remembers that he had been a Trotskyite and that his cause had been betrayed by such as McLeod who insisted on revolution in one country. None of this strange assortment of circumstances and characters is convincingly explicated or brought to life. But we can perhaps understand the appeal of McLeod for the writer. He is a man who has not only lived on the edge of experience, dangerously and excitingly. He has also held the lives of others in his hands. The Communists can always indulge the fantasy that he is playing out a necessary dialectical role in history. McLeod has killed, and should accept the consequences. He cannot, however, if he is too remote from those subsequent events. He 'came to the conclusion that to murder one's own child is the least reprehensible form of murder. For do in a stranger, and you know nothing of what lives you snarl and what grief you bestrew. But take the axe to your own brat, and the emotional price is yours alone. Murder is nothing and consequence is all.' The doctrine propagated by McLeod here is that anything is permissible provided that you stand in the full light of your own action and bear its implications. Act at each moment with your total will however it changes. And it surely will change if your are truly alive and dynamic. Early Mailer fiction presages the later existentialist.

And in a subsequent novel, *An American Dream,* the author is concerned with his hero at the point of ultimate experience. Stephen Pojack, honoured Congressman, author and television personality, murders his millionaire wife and is then tempted to suicide. This, for him, conjures up once more the experience of the war when he was likewise forced to kill. What, he asks himself, is the difference between President Kennedy (to whom he had dedicated his previous book) and himself? 'The real difference between the President and myself was maybe that I ended with too large an appreciation of the moon, for I looked down the abyss on the first night I killed.' The hero's special distinction is his personal experience of the abyss. He himself has been on the edge of life, not responsible for death at some remove. To be truly existential, man has to look into the face of death and see it. Pojack has killed. Now the expiation has to be earned by the sense of death's presence. That is when life is most meaningful: 'Comfortless was my religion, anxiety of the anxieties, for I believed God as not love but courage. Love came only as a reward.' To go through the murder and justify his existence he must challenge death. Only when he has survived the duel to come will life be satisfactory.

Mailer is not so much notable for the calibre of his writing as for the assertion of his personality in a composite literary opus. He stands as an exemplar of the new popular form known as faction, intertwining description of public events with invented material. But it would all be evanescent without the person of 'M' stalking in the undergrowth, testing the motivation of others and himself. His somewhat tenuous grounding in an acceptable social reality removes the author once more to the fringes of that society. But henceforth, these fringes can become the admired new ground of the marginal man, the hipster, the existentialist. If he writes as a Jew, it is as a Jew who is tied neither to the world in general, nor to a Jewish context. But it is precisely this lack of belongingness that constitutes the peculiar sort of heroism here.

It is difficult if not impossible for an author to keep himself out of his own fiction. But whereas Mailer thrusts himself to the fore, abandons disguises and opts for a peculiar brand of heroism, Bernard Malamud (b. 1914) tends to prefer the hero as victim, beaten up *(The Assistant),* condemned *(The Fixer),* exploited *(The Tenants),* partially impotent *(Dubin's Lives),* certainly always unhappy, not totally fulfilled, aware that things could have been better. This, in Yiddish lore, is the type of the nebish. For Malamud, it is precisely this quality that makes a Jew Jewish, and he does not have to be ethnically Jewish to play out a Jewish role. In *The Assistant,* for example, it is precisely the Gentile 'assistant' Frank Alpine, who becomes symbolically and in actuality the real Jew of the novel. At the outset, we meet Bober in considerable straits — his health is bad and business declining. As the narrator reflects: 'The world suffers. He felt every schmerz.' His destiny is predetermined, as his daughter Helen tells him: ' "With that name you had no sure sense of property, as if it were in your blood and history not to possess, or, if by some miracle to own something, to do so on the verge of loss. At the end you were sixty and had less than at thirty." ' To add to his misery, he is struck on the head, robbed in his shop. Racked by guilt, he volunteers to act as Bober's assistant and even to take his place whilst he is off sick. Alpine's attitude to Jews is ambivalent, but it often supports the implied view of the author: They were born prisoners. That's what they live for, Frank thought, to suffer. And the one that has the biggest pain in the gut, and can hold on to it the longest, without running, is the best Jew.' And he adds 'no wonder they got on his nerves'. A latent anti-Semitism is assumed, but it is an anti-Semitism that does not preclude identification with the Jewish situation. Frank worries about the Jews, not least because he is so attracted to Helen. He asks Morris why he considers himself a Jew, since he does not keep kosher, or go to the synagogue, or wear a hat, or take the Jewish holidays off work. Morris answers that being Jewish means to be honest and good. It also means to suffer for other people. Eventually, Morris dies, and the Rabbi's eulogy again asserts similar values: ' "He suffered, he endured but with hope." ' 'To suffer whilst holding on in order to suffer again, seems to be the hallmark of Jewishness. Frank, after Morris's death, takes over the supervision of the store and converts to Judaism. He undergoes circumcision. That experience informs what it is to be Jewish. It is pain.

In *The Assistant* we see the assumption of the Jewish role by non-Jew. The possibility of such substitution and role reversal is illustrated by the fable 'The Jewbird' *(Idiots First)*. Here, a skinny bird flies into the Cohens' apartment, shouting '"Gevalt. A pogrom."' This is the Jewbird called Schwartz, displaying all the accepted Jewish characteristics. Afraid of 'anti-semeets', he is now seeking refuge at the Cohens. But Cohen, resentful and jealous, wants to get rid of the bird and, eventually (in replication of the Yom Kippur atonement), flings it out of the window. When the corpse is discovered, Mrs Cohen says that it is those 'anti-semeets' who have killed it. As the bird has become Jewish, so Cohen has become the anti-Semitic persecutor.

And in *The Fixer,* based on the case of Mendel Beiles accused of ritual murder in Kiev, 1910, the Beiles figure, Yaakov Bok, takes on the historical function of the Jew. After undergoing poverty and repression, he takes up residence, illegally, in Kiev. But then comes the charge of ritual murder and the conviction. He had wanted to be freed of his Jewish yoke, but as he says to the investigating magistrate: ' "If the Jews don't mean anything to me, then why am I here?" ' He is forced into a political position against his will, and into a Jewish position in spite of himself.

The underdog of Malamud's stories and novels comes over in different forms. Arthur Fidelman of the 'Fidelman' series is a self-confessed failure in his career, in his love-life and in his luck. The central figure of *Dubin's Lives* is not a failure of such an obvious sort, and the work is a much closer representation of lived reality than Malamud's earlier tales. Dubin, a biographer, is, in fact, quite a successful writer, having won an award from the hands of President Johnson, no less, for his 'life' of Thoreau. When we first meet Dubin at the age of 56, he is engaged on a life of D. H. Lawrence. But he feels that he is now entering old age, has lost his zest for life, his sense of newness, his love for his wife. He is residually Jewish but married to Kitty, a non-Jew, and has lost any sense of Jewish connection, although it is hinted that it might be re-established through his daughter's erratic and paradoxical loyalties. The main thrust of the novel is his growing obsession with a young girl, Fanny, who initially comes to clean for the household. She revives his lust and his life. But he does not want a divorce.

As is the case with major novels, the reader has more information on which to base a judgement of the character than does the character himself, even with his considerable intellectual sophistication and introspection. Dubin, an unhappy man, might not ultimately grasp the workings of his unconscious mind. Although Dubin is grasping with lives all the time, and with great success and panache, he cannot so easily grasp his own life. As he says of himself: 'I've given up life to write lives.' His impotence represents his lifelessness. All is invested in his biographies. He himself is in the grip of depression: 'He feared illness. immobility; the   disgrace of death.' Malamud describes with remarkable virtuosity the melancholy of self-conscious ageing. Perhaps it is described better than in Dubin's own speech, which is literary, convoluted and disguised. But this phrase makes him regret lost opportunities without offering an alternative compensation in the future: 'Middle age, he thought, is when you pay for what you didn't have or couldn't do when you were young.'

Unlike Bellow, whose opus is a sort of continuing self-portrait in confessional prose, Malamud has varied his mode of writing over the years. He has produced sports stories, fables, historical fiction and detached drama. *Dubin's Lives* is the most naturalistic of his novels to date. But through all the modes, the Malamud-type hero has retained his original character —melancholy, pessimistic, basically unfortunate. And the Jewishness of the character is not dependent on his ethnic origin or social milieu. His Jewishness is rather his function in the world.

More than Trilling, Bellow, Mailer or Malamud, Philip Roth (b. 1933) presents the reader with the actual texture of contemporary Jewish life in America. Whereas Malamud has made of the Jew a functional myth and Bellow has seen the Jew as educated outsider and observer of urban society, Roth has tried to paint a portrait from the inside, suggesting what it is like to have grown up as a Jew in American society, as well as to be a Jew in the world at large. This portrait has metaphysical, ideological and social implications, but it does at least attempt to represent the material of surface life as perceived by the narrator.

This narrator is mostly an active participant in the story. There is no detachment from the action. In Roth's most successful work, the author's own experiences create the story and colour the manner. When Roth speaks from his own life and passions, the force of this experience communicates itself. When he attempts a description of the larger American society and tries to sympathise with a situation beyond his passion if not his ken, the effect fails. This has happened in *When She was Good*, which endlessly repeats the proposition initially implicit in the data of the story. The novel fails to grip because the action is not generated by the development of character. And the people therein are not individuated or seen in the round.

Roth first eatablished himself with the collection of stories, *Goodbye Columbus*. He is particularly successful in the short story form, where the character does not have to be developed over a long range. Here, reflecting the youthful preoccupations of the author, we recognise the opposition on the part of the narrator to the official line as promulgated by an establishment figure. In 'The Conversion of the Jews', the young Ozzie challenges his Rabbi/teacher. 'Ozzie suspected he had memorised the prayers and forgotten all about God,' and then says to him directly: '"You don't know anything about God."' The youngster, searching for truth, cannot tolerate pretence and hypocrisy in those who would guide him on his way. In his religious quest, the child rejects a discipline that commands obedience. He managed to extract a promise from all the authorities not 'to hit anybody about God'.

But the story 'Eli the Fanatic' is more ambivalent and subtle. A lawyer, Eli Peeke, represents a community that resents the intrusion of a Talmudical Academy into a settled, upper-middle-class neighbourhood. He is asked to persuade the director, Leo Tzuref, to move to another suburb. But strangely, Eli gradually takes on Tzuref's own external characteristics, and himself dons the traditional East-European garb. This is not just sympathy, but total self-identification. He has become the archetypal Jew in his fight, and it is he then who is rejected as mad by the regular members of the local community who initially employed him. Is personality, as its etymology suggests, a mask that covers identity, something that can be adopted or exchanged? Do we move in and out of roles, and is that what being Jewish means? The story is too cryptic to impose its own answer, and various interpretations have been suggested. A lawyer's role is also ambiguous. He represents and therefore identifies with anybody for a fee. But now, at the story's end, the blackness (darkness of the garb) had irrevocably entered his soul. He had stopped being merely a lawyer, a puppet, and was now established in a mould. The community cannot come to terms with something negative, 'black', and prefers to live on the pleasant, bourgeois surface. But this black is nevertheless a reality and a Jewish reality at that. By recognising this, Eli becomes locked into a genuine Jewish identity, associated with a fate determined by history, and is therefore, in terms of the title and observations of the community, a 'fanatic'.

A recognisable Jewish locale also marks *Portnoy's Complaint,* which takes place in the recall of Portnoy on a psychoanalyst's couch. At the stage of early middle age, the hero wants to review his own life and examine its roots. This typical American scenario can provide a suitable framework. The material from the book looks uncensored as would be appropriate in a psychoanalytic exercise whose object is cathartic. But the novel has to be seen in terms of comic irony, producing stereotypes in character, action and attitude. Portnoy is typical of rebellious youth, materially and socially successful, but rejecting the imposition of restrictive Jewish society and attitudes, The mother is over-protective, all-encompassing, stifling the child. The father is literally and metaphorically, constipated, unable to achieve contact with the son or influence him. This, the hero suggests, is what passes for Jewish life in the contemporary world. It is an environment spiritually empty, choked by the search for status. The novel is a commentary on the joke: 'My son, the doctor, is drowning.' Only here, the recurrent theme is not a joke in the sense of something unlikely and speculative. It has happened. Portnoy's home, instead of being a refuge, has become a prison. His only point of retreat is the bathroom, where he can lock the door and take his pleasure in private. This is his road to self-liberation: 'Furiously I grab that battered battering ram to freedom.'

Portnoy is an adult (thirty-three years old) who has not grown up. He needs the unlocking of analysis, because he is still chained to his mother. He cannot marry because he does not see woman as an equal, but only as a means to achieve private satisfaction. He has not matured, because his parents are still with him. So he is frozen in a childhood attitude: 'Good Christ, a Jewish man with parents alive is a fifteen-year old boy, and will remain a fifteen-year old boy till they die.' And then a later correction: 'A Jewish man with his parents alive is half the time a helpless infant.' What he wants, as he tells the doctor, is 'to put the id back in yid'. By 'id' he presumably understands a ladder to adulthood. The child cannot distinguish his ego from the rest of the world. The process of maturation sifts the ego out into a separate compartment, whence the residue of inchoate feeling (id) can be drawn upon. Portnoy has not passed the ego stage. To exemplify this, he can conquer women in America with some ease. These women are inferior to him and thus simply carry out sexual functions. In Israel though, women are aggressively equal, and Portnoy cannot relate to them sexually. The kibbutznik Naomi tells him: ' "You are nothing but a self-hating Jew." ' For all his sexual prowess, it seems that his mother has castrated him. In this novel, as in so many other diaspora versions of Israel, the

Israeli is seen paradoxically as the reverse Jew. It is paradoxical because Israel aspires to create the most complete Jew, the unhyphenated Jew that Rosenzweig posited. But the myth of the Jew as an essentially diaspora figure emerging from local conditions in a minority situation, holds good for Portnoy. He is typically trying to break out of his fetters, and enter the adult world. Philip Roth has achieved his distinction in etching versions and interpretations of the social Jew in contemporary America.

Many would question whether the encapsulating definition 'Jewish' could be genuinely applied to any of the writers discussed so far in this chapter. Although they may be ethnically Jewish, as may or may not be their characters, no issue of Judaism is raised, and they do not put accross a Jewish message. This view, however, would confine Jewish writing to writing about 'Judaism' – as a religion or ethical and legal system, and would not take account of the subtleties and variations of Jewish meaning and implication in the modern world. It is just such a straitjacket that we have tried to jettison here. However, it is indeed remarkable that so few of the unquestionably Jewish writers really try to come to terms with any form of Judaism in a historical, religious or cultural way, in fact, in any but an ethnic or social sense. Chaim Potok (b. 1929), however, is one of the few who really does try to present an understanding of Judaism as seen from different points of view.

Judaism in conflict is not a new theme in literature. The tradition has often been explicated in dialectical terms, particularly by writers who were reared in the traditional milieu and then left the orthodox fold. There is a strong Yiddish literature which represented a secularising tendency. On the contemporary scene, I. Bashevis-Singer (b. 1904) has attempted to draw the modern world with its internal conflicts and branches, particularly in his family sagas such as *The Manor* and *The Estate*. This is Bashevis-Singer in his naturalistic mode. C. Grade (b. 1910) has also portrayed the traditional world in conflict. For example, *The Agunah* ranges the forces adhering to the strictest interpretation of Jewish law against either those of a liberalising tendency or those who are subject to other forces altogether. Not only do we have intellectual strife and conflict as between faith and reason, but also as between discipline and instinct. But such material constituted the rockbed of a theme back in the nineteenth century when other winds began to blow through the Jewish world. Values could then be compared and contrasted as foreign influences made themselves felt. Enlightenment was a potent force, and the conflict resulting from its contact was drawn in a book such as the autobiography of M. Lilienblum, *Hetath Neurim* in 1876.

But whereas the Enlightenment line challenges traditional thought, Potok views it sympathetically in terms comprehensible to the outsider. In his novels, the most rigid American Judaism is challenged both by alternative sources of truth and by the 'Conservative' form of Judaism which would permit and encourage the use of scientific scholarship. *The Chosen* and its sequel *The Promise* are retailed from the point of view of the son of a modern Talmud teacher, Malter, in an orthodox suburb of New York. A surprising friendship is cemented after a hostile baseball match with a Hasidic school, when Danny Saunders, the pitcher, almost takes Malter's eye out. Danny is expected to be successor to his Rebbe father, leader of a Hasidic sect. But he displays unusual talents in many directions, and cannot narrow his horizons to the Talmudic world exclusively. Malter, of the more liberal background, wants both to graduate in Philosophy and to receive ordination for the rabbinate. *The Chosen* covers the earlier school and college period, and presents the contrasting environment and family backgrounds. *The Promise* takes the story on to the career development. The titles of the two books indicate their subject matter. The first treats the individuals as selected, whereas the second indicates the option accepted. If they are chosen by God, as are all Jews in the understanding of the tradition, the individual has to respond in mutuality, for the God-man dialogue to take place.

Both Danny and Malter have to face conflict. Danny has to break out of a rigidly circumscribed background with its well-defined expectations of him, in order to be truly himself. He starts to pick up secular information voraciously and tenaciously. But ultimately, he remains within the fold and still thinks as a Hasid. Malter, also a brilliant student, is encouraged to diversify his interests, but he aspires to the heart of the tradition, and wants to receive ordination from the fanatical Rav Kalman, recently arrived from Europe. Kalman is furiously opposed to Malter senior's scholastic method as applied to the Talmud: ' "Where do you stand? Do you stand with true Yiddishkeit, or do you stand a bit on the path of Gordon?" ' The question posed by Kalman to Malter relates to his friend Professor Gordon's 'heretical' notions of Judaism, where fundamentalism is jettisoned. Both Danny and Malter in their different ways want to hold on to both worlds totally and uncompromisingly, to remain completely committed to Judaism as well as to be familiar with every aspect of contemporary thought.

These novels, as well as the later work of Potok, suggest a synthesis of worlds. The psychology of individuals and family relationships is successfully interwoven with conflict. Although this is not the greatest of comtemporary Jewish writing, and has not the flair, brilliance, humour, imagination and unpredictability of some of our other cases, it has succeeded in bringing an awareness of Jewish issues to a contemporary audience in a palatable way. There is a somewhat monotonous and unrelievedly gloomy atmosphere in novels that read at times very much as though they are trying to illustrate a thesis, rather than be carried away by the vitality of character and plot. And they are more novels of ideas than of character in action, although they aspire to be both. But the work is still an important restatement of a perennial conflict already illuminated in earlier literature. It makes exciting reading and has a uniquely American accent.

8 ON THE FRINGES OF EUROPE: THE ITALIAN SCENE

After a two thousand year history of continuous settlement, Italian Jewry is hardly a foreign body in this, the original Latin land. In fact, it is as ancient and rooted as any other element within Italy. But culturally integrated as it is locally, this group of communities has also produced a Hebrew poetry going back twelve hundred years and a generally distinguished Hebraic/Judaic culture in all its branches. It is on the edge of Europe, to some extent peripheral in its experience, not quite so sharply and suddenly depleted by the Enlightenment, which Italy had known earlier in the form of the Renaissance, nor so totally crippled by the European holocaust. Italian Jewry was already diminutive. The figure of 40,000 or so souls did not rise in the century between 1830 and 1930, despite the general population expansion. This was the effect of the Risorgimento, in which the Jews participated so enthusiastically, tempting the Jewish population into an identification with the spirit of the new Italian nationalism.

Until the Napoleonic wars though, Italian Jews, in all of the different states where they had been permitted to settle (not, for example, in the Kingdom of Naples), were a distinct element within the realms, separated on religious grounds from the Catholics. The first ghetto was set up in Venice in 1516, and post-Renaissance Italy saw a flight of the Jews in the face of intolerance and restriction. For example, from the mid-seventeenth to the mid-eighteeneth century, the Jews of Venice declined in number from 5,000 to 1,500 souls. The climax of these deprivations was Pius VI's 'editto sopra gli ebrei' of 1775 'summarising in forty-four clauses, one more degrading than the other, all the persecutory measures of his predecessors' (Roth). But as the Austrian Empire was undergoing change, so too were Austrian possessions in Italy. Emperor Joseph II's Toleranz-Patent of 1781 offered a changed although conditional status to the Jews of the Empire. And later, another great European power, France, invaded Italy, and even occupied part of it. The French revolutionary 'rights of man' were enthusiastically embraced by Italian Jewry, which supported the invaders. Jews adopted the title of 'citizen', and the ghetto gates (literally) started to fall.

After reversals in the 1820s and 1830s, followed by the abortive revolutions of 1848, Liberalism was enthroned with the crystallisation and unification of a new Italian Kingdom in the reign of Vittorio Emannuele II, from the middle of the century. Territories were gradually incorporated into the Kingdom, including that of the greatest city and home of the most substantial Jewish community, Rome, in 1867, when it was made the capital of a united Italy.

Henceforth, so strongly aligned were the Jews with the national spirit that many joined the Fascist Party when it was founded in 1919. Mussolini's stance was generally regarded as non-racist and non-antisemitic but he did say at the third Congress in 1921: 'I want it to be known that for Fascism the racial question is of great importance. Fascists must do everything possible to maintain purity of race intact, because it is race that creates history' (Centro). With the rise of Fascism, the status of Jews changed dramatically. Communal association was made compulsory in 1930 and, from 1936, Fascism moved closer to Nazism when Germany supported Italy's invasion of Abyssinia. In 1938, racial legislation was introduced on the Nuremberg model: 'One of the most appalling features about the persecution was its suddenness. In Germany, in a soil prepared by generations of poisonous propaganda, it had taken four years to reduce the Jews to their present plight; in Italy, the same took place almost overnight' (Roth). Italy entered the war as an ally of the Nazis on 10 June 1940. But after the fall of Mussolini on 25 July 1943, Germany, rather than retreat, intensified its occupation. The bite of the snake was at its most deadly after it had been struck. It was late in the year 1943 that seizures of Jewish population took place all over Rome and North Italy. Jews were then transported to the camps. But still 'rather less than 8,000 deaths can be established among the Jews whom the Germans deported from Italy. More than five-sixths of a Jewish population estimated at about 52,000 in 1939, survived the war' (Reitlinger).

Necessarily, the literature discussed in this chapter is that of the survivors. Directly or indirectly, we will be looking at the record of this ancient community in modern times, so deeply entrenched in the life of the country, yet shaken into an awareness of separation. We are dealing with a totally Italian product, heir to an even more ancient Jewish heritage. By the twentieth century, the Jewish aspect was culturally peripheral although historically decisive. The Jewish fate was now as a human fate rather than one of ethnic, religious, specific concern. Italian Jewry, in its size and in its cultural association with the host country, was the modern trend writ large. Although smaller than many other Jewish communities, it was no less significant. It has not shared the total horror of others for a multitude of reasons, but it has been more than touched by it. And this is when its specificity enters. Full party to the splendid history of Italy, it has also another history. The literary record of Italian Jewry is no longer written even partially in Hebrew. But, in Italian guise too, whatever its overt subject, it bears those earlier markings.

In the second half of the twentieth century, the serious essay has not been much cultivated as literary genre. Perhaps its place has been taken by the omnipresent newspaper comment or editorial and by the review, both, as occasional writing, in the press. Natalia Ginzburg (b. 1916) has established, beyond the range of her novels and stories, a place for the considered and balanced statement on weighty matters (although conducted with a sureness and lightness of touch) well beyond the ephemeral. In her essays, particularly in those collected under the title *Mai devi domandarmi* (1970, *Never Must You Ask Me*), 1973, she decides, after having achieved an age beyond the reach of mundane ambitions and fluctuations of mood, to set down her mature reflections on the things that matter to her, in life, art, politics, religion, all with the stamp of her own truth.

Everything that she writes emanates from herself. Her stories too have this reflective character. As Isabel Quigly says in her introduction: 'everything she writes has so "unmistakable" a presence that it is hard not to think of everything she writes as in some way autobiographical'. Her story 'La madre' ('The Mother') has this reflective, retrospective character. The children ponder their mother's true nature long after her death. They would have preferred a mother of a different kind, one more 'motherly', less butterflyish, more like their grandmother. She was too young, too flighty, too insubstantial, too unhappy. And, of course, she was inadequate in her role as mother. But she died prematurely and tragically, by her own hand, after an unhappy affair.

Ginzburg is half-Jewish, and this seems to epitomise her status. In and out, not quite of the society that she describes, she hankers after integration and normality. But it is just such qualities that are denied her. She would have liked to be more like other children, like the people in the street: 'I should have liked a mother, who, in the evening, sewed in the lamplight. My mother didn't sew, or sewed too little for my taste. I should have liked to hear them talking about the Fatherland. No-one ever mentioned it. I should have liked to hear them talk about the king. They called him an idiot. They didn't send me to school, they made me study at home for fear of germs. I should have liked them to put a flag out on the balcony on patriotic feast days.

We had no flag' ('Cuore'). But, as one of the main stream, she can more detachedly reflect on the value of things. She is determined to avoid lies, even if that involves silence 'until we can find new, true words to describe the things we love' (ibid). In the meantime, the word is so corrupted that it must either be totally renewed or dropped. Out of step with the world around, the writer is also out of step with her time: 'To be honest, my own time inspires me with nothing but hatred and boredom' ('Collective Life'). And what can one do who is so totally at odds, perhaps not only with the particular circumstances that find her, but even with the notion of of the collective? Retreat must be sought in the self. This is her difficulty with the contemporary scene; the world presses on the single soul and allows no respite: 'Since everything that forms the life of the individual is neglected and humiliated, and the gods of collective existence are venerated and sanctified, it follows that solitary thought is not considered at all important' (ibid). The world of feeling is being obliterated, because it is too painful. Effort and labour must be reduced in the negative attempt to avoid discomfort. And as in life, so in letters, because art must follow life and exemplify it. In creativity too, there is a 'wish for non-fiction, non-labour, non-pain, non-bloodshed. The dry, confused novels and verses written today tell us that not a trace of real effort has been spent in writing them, and the author of them has merely been reflecting himself, his own dryness and confusion' (ibid). But Ginzburg's view is that life, the true substratum of the human soul, has not essentially changed. Pain still exists; it has merely been obscured. The modern apparatus of living, including drugs, acts as a drug, i.e. it does not fundamentally induce change, it rather obscures perception of the true condition. It may be that in this pursuit, unpleasantness has been reduced. But then too, so has the ecstasy. The drama and fury of life and love are no longer there, just a mechanical pleasure, an absence of extreme experience. Thus there is an overall reduction of humanity. The only expressions of man's freedom are those that are produced by his own confusion, his use of substitutes and aids rather than the life confrontation. There is a kind of freedom involved in this output of artefacts. But 'this freedom is neither proud nor gay, nor is it even desperate because it never had any hope; it has no past and no future because it has neither plans nor memories, and it seeks in the present, not a fragile happiness which it would have no idea how to use, having no imagination and no memory, but a lightning sense of survival and choice' (ibid).

So our authoress in her nostalgia and recollection of another time, also recalls a better time. Not in terms of living standards, but in terms of life itself. What we have, in her view, is not experience so much as a series of sensations. Her essays aspire then beyond the transient to something permanent, towards a standard. She yearns, paradoxically perhaps, for a critic and for his criticism, for a 'judgement that is clear, steady, inexorable and pure' ('Criticism'). But there is no true judgement involved in the act of criticism today. The role of the critic like that of the father is extinct. We ourselves once had fathers, the older generation, but we, in turn, cannot be fathers/critics: 'we shall never have our tears dried, never take over the fatherly role ourselves; it may be a simple thing, but it is impossible, inadmissible, and we continue to grope and tremble in the dark' (ibid). Only judgement is light. Or, light produces judgement.

Alberto Moravia (b. 1907), the 'maestro', is possibly the most famous and one of the most prolific contemporary fiction writers in Italy. Since the late 1920s, he has published a stream of short stories, novellas and novels, and is still actively productive. We can then only selectively highlight some of his main themes, preoccupations and techniques. The story line is always very lively and tense. The tension is created by the mystery of motivation and action, and the difference between apparent motivation and the transparent action. Motivation is fully explicated by the omniscient narrator, but the plot might belie the expectations planted.

The nature of his stories has not changed so much over the years. Ambiguity of motive is already present in *Gli indifferenti* (1929, *The Time of Indifference*, 1953). The plot revolves around the relationship of a mother, Mariagrazia, her 'friend' Lisa and her daughter Carla, to Leo, who, through his wealth and position, has some power over all of them. The mother is his mistress, but he now desires and wants the daughter. Lisa had been his mistress many years ago, and now seeks to foil his intent and the family's prospects. Carla wants to escape her life of dependence and her mother's hysterics, and so is willing to take up some sort of offer, and so achieve a 'new life'. Her brother, Michele, a weakling, tries to assume the part of jealous protector, and even makes a rather farcical attempt, following all sorts of fantasies, on Leo's life. The ambiguities are to be found in the recognition of the precise intentions and ambitions of each. Michele articulates the general doubt in respect of his own case. He worries about his lack of sincerity. He is pretending to an emotion that he does not authentically experience. Leo might be willing to marry Carla. Carla has her doubts about this new life. Her mother is clearly living a total fantasy. Lisa pretends to friendship, but is consumed by jealousy. The novel ends before a resolution in action and a tying up of the different strands.

In *La mascharata* (1940, *The Fancy Dress Party,* 1941), the title expresses this ambiguity. Man's passage in life might be through a series of disguises. The great General, Tereso, in invited to a party by a leading hostess in an unnamed South American country. He is willing to go because he hears that the lovely Fausta will be there. But Fausta is to marry the servant Doroteo. Through the juxtaposition of ambition, motive and denouncement, what had been an effort by the Chief of Police to stage a pretended attempt on the Dictator's life becomes a real killing, though of someone else. The intended wedding has become a funeral. A paradox lies in plan becoming reality, because the reality achieved differs so from the plan. What was to be the revolutionary action by Saverio turns into a farcical and futile self-sacrifice.

The two novels *'L'amore coniugale* (1949, *Conjugal Love,* 1951) and *Il depresso* (1955, *Ghost at Noon,* 1955) deal with the relationship of art to creativity. The first person narrator of the former, early in his marriage, has found not only contentment but also the satisfaction of an ongoing conjugal passion. But, not for any material motive, he aspires to a literary creativity beyond the minor though competent criticism tht he has so far managed. At first, he is convinced that he is producing a masterpiece, but then later realises its unreality (i.e. the unconnectedness of his work with his life and his wife). In spite of her lack of sophistication, his wife indicates the weakness of his story. Although it is about her, he has not known her well enough to make the story convincing. Something of the kind is indicated by the obtuseness with which he allows his barber, Antonio, to continue his visits to the house, in spite of her initially violent objections. The second novel also treats of the failure on the part of the husband to understand his wife. Again, the marriage is at first blissful, but then turns sour with his growing success as a film scriptwriter. He is dependent on the producer Battista who has become close to his wife. A parallel to the Odyssey story that he is writing is suggested. Perhaps he should behave like the ancient hero who killed Penelope's suitors. Their relationship is marked by ambiguity, even after her disastrous death and his hallucination of reconciliation: 'the ambiguity which has poisoned our relationship in life, continued even after her death'. He would like to find her again with 'renewed serenity'.

Ambiguity of motive lies at the core of *Il conformista* (1951, *The Conformist,* 1952). We have a portrait of a sadist from childhood, who, because of his tendencies, at first feels himself an outcast, as one so different. But these tendencies can be harnessed to the collective will, with the rest of Fascism. So his sadism can be made not only respectable, but commonplace. Marcello had, as a child, killed, or thought that he had killed, one Liveo, a defrocked priest, then a chauffeur, who had made homosexual advances to him. But now, as an adult in a Fascist context, he can kill respectably. After all, this is in conformity with the general will. He loves the 'people' as an abstraction, although he cannot bear the messiness of individuals. He wants to be absorbed into the totality and anonymity of the whole. But the apparent tranquillity and success of his career and life are upset by the intrusion of feeling. Just after his marriage, he conceives a genuine desire for the wife of his old tutor, Quadri, the man marked out for murder. How could he understand his actions now? 'It suddenly seemed to him acutely distressing not to know whether he was doing things because he liked them or because they suited his plans.' From then on, and until his violent death, doubt sets in.

Moravia's fictional preoccupation then since his first novel has been with the question of what is the real person. In *La ciociara* (1957, *Two Women*, 1958), the originally saintly Rosetta, so helpless, so dependent on her mother, so self-effacing and good, seems to be totally transformed by the violent rape that she suffers after they escape war-torn Rome to return to her mother's village. The simple mother narrates the events, and tries to understand this transformation. 'And I reflected later, when this impression of mine was, alas, confirmed, that during those few moments of agony my poor Rosetta had grown abruptly into a woman, both in body and mind, into a hardened, experienced, bitter woman, bereft of all illusion and hope.' But perhaps this 'new destiny' had always been latent. Do we really understand people at first assessment? Notions of 'good' and 'life' undergo modification. The good has to be tested by experience, and life persists against all logic, as signified by the resonance in the novel of the New Testament Lazarus episode.

Some of the implications of the writing discussed so far for Italian Jewry have been indirect. The masterpiece of contemporary Italian Jewish fiction is *Il giardino dei Finzi-Contini* (1962, *The Garden of the Finzi-Continis*, 1965) by Giorgio Bassani (b. 1916). Some view it as the only work of recent times to deal with aspects of Jewish life both 'with the commitment of testimony and the touch of an artist' (Milano). Through the focus of the narrator on a particular family and the recall of the Jewish cemetery in Ferrara, a substantial segment of the history of modern Italian Jewry is presented. The story is told in retrospect, as of the year 1957. The 'monumental tomb of the Finzi-Continis' is not for use any more; only one of that family known to the narrator had 'in fact achieved that everlasting repose'. This was Alberto who had died of a rare disease in 1942, the year before the transports. The tomb recalls the splendour of expectation with the civil equality granted in 1860, the prosperity of the family and its status, and by contrast, its later oblivion under Fascism and Nazism.

But this novel is not just a case history, epitomising the fate of a group. It is about a very particular and special family, and the novel seeks to characterise this family and retail its specialness. In fact, the fascination of the book derives from this distinction between 'normal' people and 'special' people. The Finzi-Continis, in their aristocratic, Sephardic separateness, one of the latter category, although the model of aristocracy was more Italian than Jewish. Particularly special was the beautiful Micòl, so loved by the narrator, but who cannot reciprocate the intensity of his passion. They are initially a race apart within the race: 'What was there in common all four of them seemed to say — between them and the distracted, whispering Italian rank and file, that even in the synagogue, before the wideopen Ark of the Lord, was still taken up with all the trivial cases of everyday life, business, politics, even sport, but never with the soul or with God?' The narrator places himself, and is placed by the Finzi-Continis, including Micòl, with that rank and file. He describes his family as the most normal conceivable: 'I myself had belonged to the G.U.F. (Gruppo Universitaria Fascista) until just now. In fact we'd always been the most normal people you could think of.' The summit of normality in the Italian context, was Fascist membership.

The Finzi-Continis had been outside all of that. It would seem that after the implementation of the racial laws of 1938, the Finzi-Continis came closer to the other Jews. They were in the same boat, after all. The 'garden' became a meeting centre for them, to replace the clubs that they were not now permitted to join. But is a mutual love between himself and Micòl a live possibility for our narrator? He would assume so from the things shared. They both value memory after all: 'for me, no less than for her, the memory of things was much more important than the possession of them'. (Indeed, the novel as a whole is like this — an intense, remote, beloved picture seen through a haze. Still, perfect, but distant.) With this in common, they should have been able to love each other. But Micòl rejects this possibility — love was as impossible with him as with a brother. And his father confirms this in a rare, confidential chat. There is something different and unattainable about the Finzi-Continis, something beyond him: 'if you married a girl like that, I'm sure it would end badly, sooner or later ... They're different ... The proverb says "wife and oxen from your own village". And in spite of appearances, that girl isn't from your own village.' In a literal sense, they are from the same place and background, from Ferrara, both Jewish. But beyond that yawns an inevitable gap that must be respected. He finally accepts the decree of distance, although he returns to the memory of her, through the concrete presence of the garden wall where they used to meet as children. In Micòl's words 'au vert paradis des amours enfantines'. The novel is a recall of the background. It is not an interpretation, because the mystery remains. But it is the presentation of that memory. Micòl had always, although foreseeing the future, preferred the present 'and the past even more, the dear, the sweet, the pious past'. The novel is about that past and the past that was then created.

Bassani is a writer who evokes intense recollections of distant episodes, and then subjects them to his own stringent analysis. The narrator in the novel *Dietro la porta* (1964, *Behind the Door*, 1972) is greatly critical of himself in this summoning up of a childhood concern. This is a book about friendship. It is located in a more distant past, during the year 1929, at the Licco. He needed to be liked by everybody, and particularly aspired to the friendship of the popular Catolica. But he also befriended the new boy Pulga, universally disliked. He is invited by Catolica to hear what Pulga was saying about him, the narrator, behind his back, from 'behind the door' in Catolica's own house. But, even after hearing the most dreadful slanders, he cannot confront the turncoat Pulga. He rather turns on his own maligned family. He later decides, and this is the burden of his terrible confession, that he had behaved less worthily than the miserable Pulga himself: 'But at that moment, while he, Luciano Pulga, was surely able to look it in the face, the whole truth, I wasn't.' That paralysing cowardice prevented him at the time from flinging the door open, and would so prevent him metaphorically for ever. He would always hide behind a door 'the same little, helpless assassin as always'. This novel too is presented through the perception of a haze of frozen memory, with its permanent statement about the present. He excavates the individual essence through an episode and its narration. Cowardice is even worse than treachery; it is an inability to be oneself truly and completely.

The borderline between fiction and memoir is inevitably fine. The prose works of Primo Levi (b. 1919) recall his terrible and dramatic wartime experiences, and his poetry reflects on them in more distilled form. The title of his famous memoir *Se questo è un Uomo* (1947, *If this is a Man*, 1960) puts the question arising out of human history's most monstrous episode. One group of people set out to obliterate the humanity of another, through total enslavement, supreme sadism and mass murder. In the face of this, two questions can be asked. One – was this effort successful? Was the human element indeed removed from those individuals so reduced? Two – is life still worth living for the survivors or the outsiders, if such deeds can be done? What is it that makes life possible and worthwhile against such brutalisation?

Primo Levi suffered this ultimate experience on his own flesh. As an Italian partisan, he was captured by the Fascist militia at the end of 1943. Then, in February of the year following, he was sent with the other Jews to Auschwitz. In epigrammatic terms, he puts down the achievement of the camps – the destruction of a man. How do we record this in words? 'Then for the first time we become aware that our language lacks words to express this offence, the destruction of a man.' Not the killing of a man, which is both easy to achieve and to record, but the destruction of a human element within the individual, which must be the result of planning and prolonged effort in the execution, and demands exquisite tension and precision in the description. Levi's book attempts to record all this, the positive doctrine of how to be, remain and never forget that one is a man. He is also reminded that he is a Jew, with a special fate and an extra human dimension: 'We collected in a group in front of their door, and we experienced within ourselves a grief that was new for us, the ancient grief of the people that has no land, the grief without hope of the exodus which is renewed every century.' The Jewish experience is constant exodus. And yet at the very nadir, on the point of despair, this despair is held off: 'Sooner or later in life everyone discovers that perfect happiness is unrealizable, but there are few who pause to consider the antithesis that perfect unhappiness is equally unattainable. The obstacles preventing the realization of both these extreme states are of the same nature; they derive from our human condition which is opposed to everything infinite.' Despair is absolute, but the human temperament adjusts to a balance, finding impairment of total perfection, but also possibilities in unlikely circumstances. A stark fact is that of the forty-five passengers transported in his carriage, only four were to survive. And this was the most fortunate of all the carriages!

What is the point of recording this bleak terror? 'We are in fact convinced that no human experience is without meaning or unworthy of analysis, and that fundamental values, even if they are not positive, can be deduced from this particular world which we are describing.' Everyone is desperately and ferociously alone in this unlikely fight for survival. In the fight, two categories are distinguished: the saved and the drowned. Extreme circumstances have reduced the former to a rare breed, marked out by health, tenacity and cunning. The Germans had their success; they succeeded in destroying the human element: 'To destroy a man is difficult, almost as difficult as to create one; it has not been easy, nor quick, but you Germans have succeeded. Here we are, docile under your gaze; from outside you have nothing more to fear; no acts of violence, no words of defiance, not even a look of judgement.' Liberation from the Germans, evacuation from the camps, also marked the slow but distinct restoration to man again. For example, bread is now shared, whereas 'only a day before a similar event would have been inconceivable'. The law of the Lager said: 'eat your own bread, and if you can that of your neighbour', and left no room for gratitude. It really meant that the Lager was dead.

But it is the sequel to this book, *La tregua* (1963, *The Truce,* 1965) that records the process of liberation and return in detail. The liberation was so thrilling and sudden, and the return so slow, painful, full of anti-climax. He is still advised to hide his Jewishness by his lawyer interpreter on the way to Katowice – 'c'est mieux pour vous. La guerre n'est pas finie.' Europe was in ruins, though it was a sort of home 'protected by a civilization which was ours'. It was permeated by 'an irreparable and definitive evil which was present everywhere, nestling like gangrene in the guts of Europe and the world'. Could there ever be normality again in these ragged lives?

In a poem 'Shema', written early in the year following the war, Levi addresses a message to the 'others', i.e. those who have not experienced this horror, about this situation. The 'shema' is the primary prayer of the traditional Jew, affirming the unity of God. It is taken from Deuteronomy, chap. VI, where Moses entreats his people to hold to the commandments of God at all times. A new entreaty is made by the poet. Ask yourself

whether this is a man,
who labours in the mud
who knows no peace
who fights for a crust of bread
who dies at a yes or a no.

As Israel is instructed to bear the words of the commandments at all stages of the day and to repeat them to their children, so are our fortunate contemporaries besought to consider the question as posed. The Biblical message has of course been secularised. It is the poet who issues the instruction rather than Moses, and the burden of his message is man's not God's. But the message is to ponder the nature of man. If we cannot note another man, we will not be noted. We become non-man. There is the New Testament echo asking us to consider whether this is a man, i.e. to behold the man. See what man has come to at the hand of other men. Could we be witnessing the components of Christ the redeemer? But the Christian language too has been secularised. Italian is, after all, the language of Humanism as well as that of the Latin church. And in this Italian poem by a Jewish writer, we are directed back to the execution of a Messiah; it is a parallel moment to the central statement of Jewish faith.

The writing discussed in this chapter is as diverse as literature itself. It is not a Jewish literature in the normal sense of being specifically Jewish, perhaps written in its own language, dealing with Jewish themes, issues of the community and so on (Milano). Even less does it treat of the large strands — such as Jewish history, contemporary Jewish existence and the place of the State of Israel for the Jewish people and the world as a whole. There are some few exceptions as in the poems entitled *Amo Israele* (1969) by Anna Maria Caredio who, as she herself puts it, converted back to the Judaism of her ancestors before they were Christianised. These poems are the fruit of various visits to Israel. They beg forgiveness for Christian sins as in the poem 'Yom Kippur di una Cristiana':

> Daughter of Zion,
> Only you can forgive, suffering one,
> Transform the names
> of Rome, Varsavia, Auschwitz,
> In lilies interwoven with incense.

But they also witness a revived Jewish nation with delight:

> One could never recall all Israel's blood and suffering,
> But now the skies have high rainbows
> Because Israel lives ('Israele è Viva').

So the difficulty of defining the Jewish element has been particularly noted with regard to Italian writing. Romano then talked about 'specific instances of the treatment of Jewish themes, in works by Jewish writers'. Whereas the difficulty is fully understandable, the terms of the analysis there take the limitation no further. Each usage begs a question. For this reason, we have tended to avoid definition altogether, even to the extent of not imposing the restraint of overt Jewish subject matter for inclusion. In various ways, we have seen the Jewish writer approach a wide range of theme in story, poem, essay, memoir and novel, which we have tried to accept on the terms of the work itself. And so the subjects have been illuminated, as all material is illuminated, by major literature.

Nevertheless, it will be observed that the scene set by the writer, even where derived from a specifically Jewish fate and condition, is generally conducted in terms of humanity in general. Primo Levi is concerned with the image of 'man' (as is the memoirist Liana Millu who underwent a similar experience). The Finzi-Continis are separate amongst the Jews, and have their own special Jewish tradition deriving from Spanish ancestry and loyalty. But their aristocratic mien is of a universal type, based on a local model. Italian Jewish literature has been an overwhelmingly Italian product since the demise of the Hebrew tradition in the very early twentieth century (Schirman). These qualifications must be noted. Although it swims in both streams, these streams are of different kinds.

9 A NEW BEGINNING: ISRAELI LITERATURE

The tendencies towards the concentration of Hebrew literature in Palestine rather than in the diaspora as described above (Chapter 5) were further confirmed by Israeli statehood. A sovereign Jewish state with a growing population offered a homeland to the Jews of the world. Meanwhile, the diaspora was reeling from the holocaust which had virtually finished off European Jewry. And the two remaining substantial communities were disappearing as cultural entities − in the Soviet Union under pressure of prohibition and discrimination, and in the United States through natural assimilation. Israel became the sole particularist source of Jewish expression. Hebrew was the official language and Hebrew literature nationally encouraged. Book production was to leap forward, particularly in the years following the declaration of the State, when the population increased so massively. Between May 1948 and December 1951 the immigration figure was 684,201 (Encyclopaedia Judaica), indicating the way that the balance of world Jewry was tilting towards residence in Israel (although even today only a quarter of it actually lives there).

Israeli writers sought to match the radical reorientation of Jewry and Israel with a new spirit in literature. It had, in this view, to be different in kind as well as in degree. After all, Hebrew literature was now the expression of an independent people in its own land, not the interest of small groups in foreign countries where Jews were but a tolerated minority. There was now a total unit, expressing a national interest, not a specialist religious or ethnic interest within a larger complex. So there were new responsibilities implied for policy making and the formation of a mature and all-embracing outlook. Just as we witnessed a sense of self-characterised distinction on the part of immigrant Palestinian Hebrew writers from their predecessors, the new Israeli writers perceived themselves as distinct from pre-Israeli writers. They wanted to invest Hebrew literature with a Sabra (native-born Israeli) character in outlook and form of expression. Their written language was also the language spoken, and they were flourishing in a condition of national normality.

The new periodical literature reflected this tendency both in its programme and its contents. Within, there were political and literary disagreements that had a common perception of itslef as 'Israeli' (even

142

if established and functioning before independence) rather than just Hebrew. Even the names of the journals suggest this view — *Alef*, i.e. the first letter of the Hebrew alphabet, implying a new beginning. The first issue of the journal was brought out in Tel-Aviv in 1949, appearing at very irregular intervals, serving as a forum for the most radical interpretation of Israelism as an entity separate from the Jewish world at large. Their ideology was popularly known as 'Canaanism', indicating its supposed hankering after a pre-Israelite tradition in the Land, and its focus on the land rather than on any particular ethnic group. It was thus a non-Jewish ideology except in the incidental sense that it was the Jews who were coming to Palestine, and reading as well as writing this literature. *Yalqut Hareim (The Comrades' Knapsack)* was also a pre-State journal which was issued intermittently between 1942 and 1946. Round it gathered some of the so-called Palmach generation, a pioneering group aggressively nationalist but left-wing, collectivist, consciously anti-fascist. Under the tutelage of Moshe Shamir, it advocated doctrines drawn from Socialist Realism. We will not, he insisted, have in the place of the old 'a literature that is naive, sweet, hackneyed, pleasant, but one that is realistic and revolutionary, a literature without mercy' (*3*, 1946). The literature was to be non-revolutionary in technique, but revolutionary in the sense that it was attached to the political and social process. A third journal, *Liqrath*, rather short-lived (1952-3), was more exclusively literary, eschewing narrow or specific political attachments. But here too, the title (meaning 'towards') suggested newness and a potential rather than tradition. It saw itself, mainly under the guidance of poets like N. Zach, M. Dor, Y. Amichai and A. Sivan, as open to possibilities of development in the light of the contemporary need. The contributors were particularly young, mainly students, less self-consciously Israeli in the political sense, cultivating a non-political verse, one generally in which the image was to predominate.

Soviet literary ideology is indirectly perceptible in *Yalqut*. A statement of Shamir's calls for a total exposure of the writer to the public and a sharing of all subject matter. Away with privacy and darkness: 'There is no life in the world other than our everyday life, no such thing as nice life or life not so nice, nice pains or pains not so nice, beautiful words, or words not beautiful, nice instincts or instincts not nice, nice subjects or subjects not nice. There is no hiding place, no dark corner in man's life that does not demand expression' (*3*). The writer is not a privately suffering individual but a public property, and he has a responsibility to his own generation. This is the Soviet docrine of the writer's responsibility to the public, although of course in the Soviet Union, the public is represented by the Party so that the writer has to articulate the Party line too. The writer also has to express a vision, i.e. to be optimistic, to believe, to be positive, not to submit to negativity or despair. The writer's function is to proclaim the revolutionary, Zionist doctrine. Zionism, goes another statement, represents 'a vision of redemption ... belief in the brotherhood of nations and men' (*4*). What then should the content of contemporary Hebrew literature be? Acceptance of pioneering doctrine, without which Hebrew literature is decadent: 'Fields and roads are the imperative of Hebrew literature, more than that, new Jewish man, his life resolution.'

Alef is less revolutionary on the Soviet model, but also less accepting of the prevalent line. It criticises Mapam (the left Zionist party) and *Yalqut* by implication, for blind acceptance of Soviet policy: 'That party's attachment to Israel is mysterious. Why should it not like the Bund, work for a Jewish socialist elsewhere? (January 1950). Participants in *Alef* include the poets A. Kenan and A. Amir, who insist on the right of those who live in the Land to shape it as they would like and to select any appropriate direction, the fictionist, B. Tammuz, who published his first stories here, and the leading ideologue of the movement, the poet Y. Ratosh, who initiated an Oriental-sounding Hebrew poetry (although he himself was from Eastern Europe). They insisted on Hebraism rather than Judaism and spoke of 'a new beginning' in an article 'We are Starting from Alef' (*1*, 1949). The destiny of the country should be determined by its inhabitants 'without regard to religion, community or origin, and in recognition of the character of the people living in Israel as distinct from the Jewish population in general'. And in another article: 'the centre of the young Hebrews (the name they gave themselves) sees the State of Israel not as a Holy Land but as a separate people, as a sovereign nation, part of the greater Hebrew land and precursor of the Hebrew renaissance overall — a national, secular renaissance, non-religious and non-sectarian.' It is because public policy is not of this colour, but instead exclusivist, sectarian, zealous in its sole loyalty to Jews that *Alef* launches its attack. It assumes that the Hebrew state's nature will be easily and readily accepted as dominant by all peoples in the region. The literary loyalties of the journal are also to characteristically Sabra literature, native to the Land, and it is critical of extraterritorial attachments. It particularly promotes the fictionist S. Yizhar, and enjoys Hazaz's fictional attack on traditional Jewish attitudes.

Liqrat promoted the avant-gardist, imagist poetry that Amichai, Zach, Dor, Sivan and company were beginning to write. In stencilled sheets, these poems were promulgated and defended by expositors such as B. Hrushowski. The tone of the journal is less strident and confident than that of the other two, more hesitant and lyrical. The subject of the verse is more likely to be personal.

We see something of the sectarianism of Israeli life in these young journals which were conducting internecine struggles along the lines of earlier Hebrew periodicals. But overall, they characterise the interests of the participants in all, their self-perception as Israeli, their different attachments and outlooks.

The periodicals issue the programme, make the statements and provide platforms for the younger writers. But we can only really gauge the full extent of their talents in the published volumes of work. M. Shamir (b. 1921) for example, established himself as an exponent of Sabra fiction with three novels, published between 1947 and 1951, i.e. during precisely that period in which Israel was struggling for its existence, emerging as an independent State, and embarking on the task of integrating a mass Jewish immigration from the world over. The author had already announced his programme for Israeli literature. It should reflect the revolution taking place in public life rather than the need to be innovative in technique. Shamir is not innovative, and produced three very traditional narratives with a hero at the centre of each one, a strong plot full of external events, and an articulated morality reflecting the prevalent attitudes in the country. The hero of the Shamir novel is the type of Sabra that has become a cliché over the years. Uri Cahana, in *Hu Halakh Basadoth (He Walked in the Fields)*, is strong, attractive, not self-analytical or over-reflective, and relates totally to the evolving situation in such matters as agriculture, security and his own growing manhood. He believes in collective responsibility as a comrade (the name of Shamir's journal). Unlike his father, Willy, who selected the kibbutz option over the other alternatives, Uri has no options. He develops in the situation into which he is born. Israel is a datum, the kibbutz is a datum, early death is a likelihood too. The typical Shamir hero dies young out of a sense of necessity and acceptance of his role. All these things are taken for granted.

Bemo Yadaw (With his own Hands) opens with the remark that 'Elik was born from the sea'. Although the context is jocular, the sentiment is genuine and generalised. The Sabra hero comes from somewhere else entirely. He is new in Israel, and yet has no roots elsewhere. He no longer has any connection with the diaspora, with a Jewry beyond, with its languages, its history and landscapes. He belongs here in Israel, but he has to suffer hostility and estrangement. The titles of Shamir's novels (and of other young contemporary Hebrew works, by such as Tammuz, Megged and Yizhar) stress the physical nature of the body against the Israeli landscape. Elik is from the sea, is very close to the animals, plants, and also the artefacts of the developing environment. So close is the Sabra to his native earth that he becomes one with it. Natural sentiment becomes his ideology. In *Thahath Hashamsh (Beneath the Sun)*, Aharon seeks to relate to his beloved Balfouria as he has done to the landscape. The author's insistence on detailed environmental description constitutes a claim to possession. The inevitable although premature death is also a very physical fact that takes place 'beneath the sun'. In contrast (as in *He Walked in the Fields)* is the Sabra-like Willy, Uri's father and his girlfriend, Mika. These are not quite native, although, in a sense, they are more admirable in that they opted to come, to remain and to be part of the local territory.

It must be obvious to the reader that such fiction is, in its way, making a point. The new Israeli literature, like the new Israeli hero, is set off as a counterpart to an older Jewish literature and hero. For the first time in centuries, in millennia, the Jew is at home in his own land, one which he has to defend from mortal enemies with his own hands and body. He loves the land, learns it , and gets to know it. He is not a man of books (there is hardly the time, and that is not the urgent need), nor is he a cosmopolitan (he belongs here and only here). He is not an introvert, because if he questions too much he may come up with the wrong answer or express doubt, when what is needed is cool decisiveness. This is the nature of the Jewish revolution, where the traditional Jewish stance, learned, passive, unrooted, is to be reversed. A new Jewish type is needed for the changed circumstances of emergent independence. This is what is meant by the revolution in life, matched by a public, celebratory, participating literature. What is needed is a healthy, positive, unneurotic attitude. This can be absorbed even by a diaspora man such as Willy, unlike Goren in the same novel, who lived a rich inner life. We need the type, suggests the narrative, who can revel in public life and set a public example. The narrative technique is traditional, with the end prefigured in the title or in the mood established at the beginning. It is also a young literature, about young people, with young attitudes.

The 'youth' of this literature is one of its problems. It became fixed in a posture which was too firm to allow later divergence. Another prose writer, and the most talented of the group is S. Yizhar (b. 1916), whose work, whilst more experimental than Shamir's, is narrower in perspective and more limited in scope. Yizhar started writing stories in 1938, publishing mainly in Lamdan's journal, *Gilyonoth*. They reflect the life of his Palestinian environment, the countryside, the animals, the kibbutz. In 1950, he produced a collection of four stories, *Arbaah Sipurim,* written over the course of two to three years, about the war in which he participated. Then he published an enormous novel, *Yemey Tziqlag (Ziglag Days,* 1958) also about the war, and another volume of stories, *Sipurey Mishor (Stories of the Plain,* 1964) about childhood, since when, virtually nothing. But a description of Yizhar's stories as being about the kibbutz or about the war or about childhood, is rather misleading. These external subjects lead him back to one focus, the reflecting consciousness. This consciousness reflects on a moral dilemma — to return to the lucerne, to release the Arab prisoner, to let the horse go, etc. (issues in his stories). After an internal struggle conducted by means of monologue, the reflector then either adopts a course of action, usually to fit in with the demands of the group, or he leaves the situation open. The monologue as argument can then continue in the mind of the reader.

There is almost no plot in a Yizhar story whatever its length, and no development either. Although argument takes place, pros and cons, weighed up against each other, the character does not undergo transformation or maturation. The argument is conducted in a language unparalleled in its range. The observation too is striking — reflector set off against the landscape, in contrast to it, quarry within the landscape, merging in it (whether horse or prisoner). Then there is the group over against the quarry and the landscape, confronting the reflector, insensitive, conformist, imposing of norms. There are four characters in a Yizhar story — the 'I', the group exerting pressure, the quarry, perhaps a sentimental projection of the 'I''s sympathy, and the language, inhuman but precisely etched. Landscape, flora, fauna, sounds of battle, conversations of soldiers, consciousness of individuals and, above all, the consciousness of the main figure or reflector, are all described intensely. But the plot does not move on. It revolves on its axis, and the situation remains much as when the story opens, although now the options have been exhaustively presented, and this 'I' can make his decision. However, decision is the thing that he will not make effectively.

The war of independence is the most effective catalyst of

conscience. If Yizhar's earlier stories had turned on a moral dilemma posed to the hero, the war could pose such a dilemma constantly and in much sharper form. For all the lack of action, there is a great passion in each sentence of the prose to establish the precise character of the landscape or the individual mood. But all the individuals are similar. They are in fact aspects of the collective, and when individuated, they are not so different from the reflector. Just as the individual does not really develop and the plot does not take the story forward, so the characters are not separated. We have a brilliant exposition of a static situation, felt, analysed and left. For this reason, the author is stranded in adolescence, from which he cannot move forward. It is interesting that his late stories take him back to childhood, and he does not get beyond the 'story that did not begin' (the title of one of his stories). The world of childhood and the author's world of primal truth, where the ego remains exclusive and pained, where no-one from the outside can share the narrator's hurt. But the converse also holds true, because the author cannot really extend his sympathy to other characters and so build up a story which takes account of differences and developments. The imagination is stunted, and thus left to fend off a situation that has already been explored. Yizhar's opus is a virtuoso work 'on one string', as Kurzweil, the Israeli critic, described it.

Hebrew poetry derives much of its power from conducting a dialogue with its own sources. Hebrew literature over the ages, with its linguistic material, has been the cloth out of which new items are cut; Biblical and, to some extent, Rabbinic sources served the metrically innovative medieval Hebrew poets in their search for both the religious inspiration and the appropriate language for occasional verse. Such has been the nature of a tongue not used in normal conversation, but that possessed a powerful literary ancestry.

And this is true even of Israeli poetry, using a language now spoken. Hebrew has only quite recently (relative to its history) been resurrected as a vernacular, and the principal echo of Hebrew cadences must derive from its tradition, a tradition of Jewish history and Hebrew liturgy. Israeli Hebrew poetry is written against the backdrop of recent wars, of the European holocaust, of a state of continuing siege, of an apparently very changed contemporary situation casting shadows sideways and backwards on to disconcerting resemblances. The Israeli poet, in commenting on the present, focuses too on his past. Y. Amichai (b. 1924), born in Wurzburg, relates with self-revelatory intensity to himself and his own story, but thus also to the story of the Jews. For it is developing Israel that he has experienced since 1936, in the shadow of the Europe which his family left. That personal watershed reflects also the moving contour of Jewish life, old Jewish diaspora, or, to give it its religious name with the negative connotation, exile. He left it to create history anew in the self-determining, emergent Israel.

Amichai delineates the tension of this situation through constant counterpoint. His particular trick, both in poetry and in prose, is the unexpected juxtaposition of the disparate images from contrasted spheres. His poems do not usually develop dialectically or lineally. They consist of allusion and picture to indicate the mood. His is a divided soul, drawn sometimes in two opposite directions, as he himself depicts that movement, upwards and downwards, heavenwards to the traditional home of God, earthwards in the direction of mundane concerns. 'They call me', from a recent collection, reads:

'Taxis below
And angels above
Are impatient.
At one and the same time
They call me
With a terrible voice.
I'm coming, I am
Coming,
I'm coming down,
I'm coming up!'

Quite commonplace in Amichai's work is proximation of the modern mechanical with the ancient spiritual, both laying claims on the narrator's attention. Using a similar image to capture the effects of his father's 'actual' death in narrative (from the story 'Deaths of my Father' in *Baruah Hanoraah Hazoth*) he writes: 'Once they called on God for help, now they call for a taxi.' And in a poem, 'Laem' ('To the Mother'), he likens the mother's dual function to a windmill's with two arms extended upwards in prayer, 'crying to heaven', and two downwards for cooking 'to prepare slices' (*Shirim*, Poems). Perhaps the principal source of Amichai's immense popular appeal, and an argument for the centrality of his verse on the Israeli literary scene, is the dramatic colour with which he has invested this theme; the effect of a functionally dead though not so distant past on a present which has been shaped by that past. Thus Amichai can embody the collective experience of a generation in his own life which he presents to us in his writing. The past may no longer be vital in its original sense, but it still grips, if with a different hold. Is God dead? Well yes, He may be, but His corpse is still with us. Another short poem, 'God's Fate' *(Selected Poems)* reads:

> 'God's fate
> Is now
> The fate of trees rocks sun and moon.
> The ones they stopped worshipping
> When they began to believe in God.
> But He's forced to remain with us
> As are the trees, as are the rocks
> Sun, moon and stars.'

A question that can be asked about the specific tensions of Hebrew poetry overall and about Amichai's poetry in particular is whether any translation can convey the original flavour. So much of this experience is locked into the Hebrew language, where the allusion of nostalgia is located in quotation, where the Hebrew faith has a textual citation. Amichai's success in other languages has surely established this possibility. He presents nostalgia which is universal — a dead though active faith is a common experience in the world today. Jewish history in its primary outlines is well-known and Amichai's type of idiom is familiar to the contemporary world. The poet's loose rhythms, bold metaphors and fleeting echoes can be well captured through the medium of another language. With all its allusive strength, the language is close to the 'language of the street', simple and idiomatic. However, examination of a single, brief poem will show us how misleading the apparent likeness of simplicity can be. An early poem, 'Geshem Bisdeh Qrav' ('Rain on a Battlefield') as represented in the published translation, reads:

> 'It rains on my friends' faces,
> On my live friends' faces,
> Those who cover their heads with a blanket.
> And it rains on my dead friends' faces,
> Those who are covered by nothing.'

The Hebrew is very simple, using no word that is uncommon in everyday speech. But the differences of the English version are manifold in their departure from the literal original. 'It rains' is a common   locution in English, whereas the Hebrew word order is at least worthy of note. 'Rain falls' is the Hebrew, whereas 'falls rain' would be the more frequent usage. The word 'friend' in the translation represents the Hebrew 'rea', which, as we have seen in the discussion of Shamir's work, has the sense of 'neighbour' or 'comrade', one not necessarily a friend, of even an acquaintance, but one bearing a common fate. It has echoes of 'And thou shalt love thy neighbour as thyself'. An oddity of the Hebrew verse is omitted in the English where the second and fourth lines conclude with the relative pronoun 'which' or 'who', thus imposing stress on a word which would not normally sustain such attention. This, in the Hebrew, puts the lines following, i.e. the third and fifth, into sharp focus. The English version has a full stop at the end of the third line, whereas, in the Hebrew, there is just a hyphen linking the two parts. The ongoing sense of the 'fading' Hebrew original thereby created is also buttressed by the last word of the poem 'od', meaning 'more' or 'longer', which in the translation is not rendered at all. This word too does not normally bear such stress in Hebrew. But the most significant difference of all comes in the shift of subject in the last line. The Hebrew is literally rendered 'who do not cover any more', i.e. the 'comrades' are no longer covering their heads with blankets, because they are dead. The simple precise observation by the poet of the special distinction between life and death, here, on the battlefield, is neutralised in the English version to the passive voice. In the English, it is not the comrades who are doing, or rather not doing, anything. It is the rain which instead stands out as the chief subject. So a very considerable shift is subtly applied in translation which totally transforms the specificity and focus of the Hebrew original. So here we have noted six significant departures from the original in a five line (24 word) poem.

This difficulty is illustrated by a poem distinguished in brevity, simplicity of language and universality of theme. If, even within such confines, the margin of difference is so wide, one can imagine the gap when a poem deploys language denser, alludes to a situation more local or to a historical connotation more complex. Amichai is a relatively easy poet to translate, but even when he writes material in a language apparently (though superficially) close to slangy vernacular, it is transformed in English translation. The English language does have a tendency to express itself at a lower voltage in any case, but the subtle nuances of oddity, stress and variation must appear, if that sense of the original is to be conveyed. In Walter Benjamin's view, the target language should be to some extent modified within the course of a successful translation, and forever changed in a historic translation. Amichai's language is misleadingly close to everyday English.

Amen is a translated selection of Amichai's poems produced in the wake of the 1973 war, opening with seven laments for the fallen. The poetry's strength is its ability to bear the direct imprint of private (but shared) experience and convey it in simple, matter-of-fact language, lifted by paradoxical images. The point of the poem is usually the irony of the life lived, the golden dream contrasted with the disappointing and necessary conclusion. 'Potatoes' are 'mashed' by the child into a 'golden puree'. Nothing more romantic in these childish dreams. But then comes death. History, public and personal, is Amichai's material and that means, for him, the record of wars. The poet's function is to seal the record, although the recorder himself may, with the wind of time, be more anonymous than the matter recorded. As the original Hebrew title has it, perhaps 'behind all this a great happiness is hiding'. But only perhaps.

How does one localise experience? Symbol attempts it. A flag stands in place of a nation. But, says the poet, 'a flag loses contact with reality and flies away'. Things change their function. The sand played with by the child now fills bags for defence. Loves are measured by war days. And the really big symbols too only have significance as symbols, not as the things they are supposed to represent. Jerusalem, that focus of history and sentiment, is only remembered as a place where 'we remember that we've forgotten something, but not what we've forgotten'. These poems are about the pain of existence and one's ('ours, the poet's') attempt to assuage it. So 'people use each other/ As a healing for their pain . . . hold each other and won't let go.' In his spiritual autobiography, *Travels of a Latter-Day Benjamin of Tudela,* he describes his passive possession by the land, not his active cultivation of it:

'I did not kiss the earth
When they brought me, a child, to this country.
But now that I have grown upon it
it kisses me
it holds me
it clings to me in love
with its grass and thorns, sand and stone
with its wars
and with its spring
until its last kiss.'

The stories of Amos Oz (b. 1939) hover on the wavering border of the natural and the surreal. His first stories and novels, set mainly either in a kibbutz or in Jerusalem, have appeared over the years since 1962. But the novel *Touch the Water, Touch the Wind** in 1973 attempted to breach the confines of the actual. On closer examination, even his naturalistic work is revealed to be not quite a straightforward representation of everyday reality. *Elsewhere Perhaps* (1966) is not just a story of life set on a kibbutz. So the charge of distortion levelled against him is no longer appropriate. After all, it is hardly relevant to accuse someone of not transmitting things as they normally occur, if that is not what he was trying to do in the first place. The bizarre denouement of the novel would bear this out.

My Michael (1968), too turns out to be not simply a record of a young marriage against the backdrop of Jewish Jerusalem. At least as significant as the overt action is the submerged fantasy. The geological image is paramount. What happens beneath the surface determines the fate of the surface itself. The husband, Michael, is a geologist, and the wife, Hannah, who tells the story, is subject to uncontrollable impulse and to seething fantasy which can spill over into her waking, social life, to the infinite perplexity of her apparently more prosaic and sober spouse.

Touch the Water, Touch the Wind differed in that it had no aspirations to naturalism at all. The primary level of the story is fantastic. The genre is the fairy tale. Amazing events are recounted and miraculous transmutations occur. So the final development, in which all the active participants are swallowed up in an earthquake in northern Israel on the eve of the Six Day War is not incongruous. The initial data placed the story beyond the bounds of the 'realistic'.

The stories that are closest to actuality are the three novellas in *The Hill of Evil Counsel* (1976). To achieve the naturalistic effect, the author seems to summon up his own childhood recollections of family life in the last years of mandatory Palestine. Here, not only is the background historical (actual personages and occurrences of the period), but everything related could be a literal representation of events as they took place. But there is the mixture as before. As the surrealistic and fairy-tale elements are conveyed in quite a matter-of-fact manner elsewhere, so the realistic elements are pervaded by subterranean tremors. Characters in the stories bear antennae picking up waves of threat and danger. We cannot forget here that the events

*As the works of Oz itemised here have all appeared in English translation, I am giving only the English titles, whilst quoting the date of Hebrew publication.

take place in Jerusalem, a city divided in loyalty soon to be divided politically. In the title story, the father's, and so the family's, house is on the frontier of no-man's land. As in *My Michael,* the woman (the mother) gives expression to the sharpest discontent and as in *Elsewhere Perhaps,* she ups and unexpectedly leaves the family. It is the woman who articulates the daemonic and the hostile, or, in general terms, 'the other'. She says to her husband in such a moment of rage: 'I want you to know once and for all how much I loathe, yes, loathe your Wertheimers and Bubers and Shertoks. I wish your terrorists would blow them all sky high.' Hannah in *My Michael* has a recurrent fantasy of the two Arab children, known to her from childhood, becoming terrorists and actually launching a raid.

But there is again the obsessionalism. In spite of the quieter representation of reality, we still have the ambiguity of Israel/Holy Land, Jerusalem as actual city and as idea/ideal. The father lives in Jerusalem, fulfilling his old-age desire. But he writes in his journal: 'I have been living in Jerusalem for three years, and I continue to yearn for it as though I were still a student in Leipzig.' We see that not only are Oz's stories a mixture of reality and fantasy, but that the characters in them find it difficult to separate these elements. He is in Jerusalem but is it Jerusalem? And if it is, which Jerusalem? Can he ever really be there? Will he ever truly and finally arrive? Most of the story takes place at a May Ball in the High Commission on the Hill of Evil Counsel. And the atmosphere of the Ball, like the story itself, is full of foreboding.

Things, we feel, and indeed as we are informed, are about to collapse: 'The last days of Rome must have been like this, Father thought to himself.' And it is at this Ball that, in conversation with Madame Josette, he is told: 'You have been leaving Europe for Palestine for forty years now. You will never arrive. At the same time, we are moving away from the desert toward Europe, and we shall never arrive either.' No desire is completely realisable. Even when we seem to be implementing a specific project, we can miss the point. Perhaps we misdefined the ideal in the first place, so the reality of fulfilment is not what we are led to expect. And meanwhile, threat is imminent. The story ends with the father attending such counsel (despair?), the mother going off with an admiral picked up at the Ball, distractedly reciting Polish verse. And the great event is the one not recorded, the one about to take place: 'On the hills around Jerusalem, the enemy set up concrete pillboxes, bunkers, gun sites. And waited.'

This story, like the other two in the volume, is concerned with the balance between appearance and reality, between things seen and things unseen. Oz's prose in its earliest stages attempted to render the force of the invisible, the lurking danger. But the later work is starker, and this volume is emotionally the sparest so far and, in narrative terms, the most representational. The events recorded are either explicitly (in 'Mr Levi') or implicitly (in 'The Hill of Evil Counsel', a third-person narrative where the child Hillel is the principal source of impressions) the summoning-up by the adult of childhood recollection. That period, 1946-7 in Palestine, has left its indelible imprint, not so much defined by what it was in itself, as by what it implied with what was to follow. The first story ends with th enemy waiting. 'Mr Levi' is also concerned with the borderline of fantasy/actuality that so preoccupies the author. Mr Levi of the story is someone who, so his parents assure the child narrator, does not exist. Is he the underground leader whose tracks must be covered or is he the product of an overwrought, childish imagination? The child is very taken up with his own projections of self-grandeur, undergoing torture and achieving heroism in the national struggle. There is the constant suggestion of great things beyond and in store. A poet called Nehamkin is a frequent guest of the family. 'All seemed to him to be hinting at an important event that was due.' In Oz's stories, poets, prophets and preachers often voice the unexpressed fears and hopes of the other characters, crystallise them with greater certainty so that their contours stand out sharply. The author seems to be writing about the past, as in a literal sense he is. But these concerns overflow into the present. In fact, past, present and future can all merge confusingly.

'Longing' is the third story, but the narrator (the old Dr Nussbaum who is writing letters to Dr Hermione Oswald on her way to America) indicates that his 'longing' is not for the future but for the past. In his case indeed, there is no future because he is terminally ill. But he might have an impersonal vision of the future for Jerusalem. Or, for the young Uri, or, indeed, for Dr Oswald – if she receives his letters as she probably will not. He does not know exactly where she is or where to direct them. Perhaps these letters are really for himself? A sort of confession. A diary? Indeed, the status of the story is uncertain and it is the least satisfactory of the three.

Oz's fiction is not only substantial in extent. It is also one of the rare attempts made by an Israeli narrative writer at some sort of encompassing vision of Israel's situation. But it is a situation seen both in its historical context and in its Jewish perspective and, also personally, through the lives and experiences of the characters and narrators. The author is looking for a thematic and psychological link between the personal and the national sphere, where split emotion not only reflects the larger picture, but is also part of that scene. There is a synthesis between the personal drama and the drama of the subject matter, the land and the people. And we have not only a vitality of character and plot, but also their illumination.

Although it is difficult to generalise across a literature, we can observe an overall change in the atmosphere of Israeli writing in the 30 or so years of its functioning. The first stage of Israeli literature was marked by a consciousness of its special role as handmaiden to the new State, either in support of a Zionist programme or in opposition to its implementation. Forces were arrayed in alignment on either side of the barricades, and writers took up open positions. But some younger writers started to beat a retreat from the public sphere into the lyrical and personal. Early prose either supported or echoed the general theme, but in the later 1950s and early 1960s, fictionists started to portray figures who consciously fled national commitment. This sort of theme is characteristic not only of writers who came to prominence at that time, but also of those who began to write earlier. Shamir's later work, for example, is of a very different character from the early novels that we described. He first took to historical themes, then assayed a sort of existential novel, *Hagvul (The Border,* 1966) where he also makes a hero in flight the central figure.

The Hebrew novel became rather more experimental in the late 1960s and 1970s. Novels were written from many points of view (Yehoshua), or told by sub-narrators or disguised narrators (Megged). The oblique influence of European events found expression in the writings of A. Appelfeld, who could also invoke the decadence of pre-war central Europe through a description of a holiday resort trying to ignore the Nazi presence, in 'Badenheim, Ir Nofesh'. Y. Kenaz has given us grotesque horror in two novels and a novella: far removed from the official, political theme. And Dan Ben-Amotz writes a sort of improvised, confessional prose, funny, slangy, iconoclastic. Poetry, since the Israeli phase began, other than that of Greenberg and N. Alterman, has generally eschewed public address and, following the Anglo-Saxon tradition, has tended towards the lyrical. The stories and novellas of A. Kahana-Carmon are poetic in this sense, intensely personal to the point of mystical communion or solipsism.

One of the most interesting experiments in the Israeli novel has been Yaakov Shabtai's *Zikhron Dvarim (Memory of Things).* We have other evidence of the author's talents in an earlier collection of stories, *Hadod Peretz Mamriy (Uncle Peretz Takes Off)* and a play called *Okhlim*, where he manages to mingle the far-fetched, the whimsical, the tragic and the satirical. Here we attend the fortunes and reflections of three friends, Goldmann, Tzazar and Yisrael over a period of nine months between (as the first few lines point out) the death of Goldmann's father and Goldmann's own suicide.

Rare indeed is the comic novel on the current Israeli scene, but especially rare is the type of comic novel that Shabtai has produced here. Making no concessions to the reader, the novel consists of but one extended paragraph. It is a kind of consciousness novel, but neither of one single stream nor emanating from a single reflector. The narrative darts constantly from one character to another, with their tales, and sub-tales, from their histories to their current activities, from their thoughts and preoccupations to their frenzied actions or impotence, and through it all there is the gnawing sense of life's oddities and overall pointlessness. *Zikhron Dvarim* is a tragic-comic novel told as a sort of swallowed sentence.

All-pervasive is the atmosphere of the book's opening, with the throwaway mention of the two deaths. The novel is about death, telling of life to illustrate the point that the most intensely imagined vitality, expressed in eating, fornicating, learning or whatever, is only an irrevelant distraction. Goldmann's dictum is that 'life is nothing but a journey into death . . . and more — that death is the essence of life fulfilling itself in it towards a final fulfilment like the chrysalis becomes a butterfly, which being so, everyone should get used to the acceptance of death, which never comes too early.' For all the preponderance of exuberant and extravagant fun, the novel is totally bleak. The only processes conveyed are the inevitability and ugliness of aging and degeneration, the transitory nature of personal attachment (no-one seems able to express genuine love) and the incapacity of anyone to rise above the action. Art in the form of Yisrael's organ playing, is invoked, particularly in times of stress. But this also fails.

Goldmann embodies the doctrine of intentional death. Yisrael and Tzazar are left to look on. Tzazar, about whom more is related in the book than anyone else, is the one to observe the coincidence of the two deaths and the nine months intervening. His own life is a catastrophe, a tide against which he swims frenetically, with his numerous affairs, frenzied pursuits and changes of activity and interest. His son is dying of leukemia, but his angry reaction to this arbitrary illness seems to induce only greater anti-life sentiment, as he forces his mistress Tehilla to undergo an abortion. He sees life only 'as a distressing and meaningless humiliation, or as a great puzzle from which one must take as much pleasure as possible'. In sober or regretful moments, he labels this attitude 'gay suicide'.

Not that there are may principles embodied in the novel. Ideals did once exist, is the thrust, though they seem now to have lost their validity. Experience has obliterated them. One sees what has transpired in a world without God. There is nihilism. Goldmann accepts the implications. But his effort to achieve a religious viewpoint ends in failure. The only purpose of life should be to try to look death squarely in the face. Not that he does not desire eternity, but he spends his time reconciling himself to the inevitable, which has become an obsession.

This novel can be read as a social critique. Here is Israeli society populated by the post-religious Jew, floundering in the enticing, open, unchartered sea of the world. His capacity to swim in it is both limited and inevitably doomed. Life is a crazy game. The rider is on the wall of death which the reader knows must collapse. Goldmann, presumably the novel's chief figure, is the most conscious of this. Tzazar is constantly trying to avoid the necessary conclusion and so gets involved in his promising but self-defeating and self-deflating adventures. Yisrael is the most enigmatic of the three, living in the shadow of the other two. He tries to find comfort in music, to change his lifestyle. But he cannot. In fact, all options are imaginary, as Goldmann would argue. Paradoxically, suicide is the only freedom. Death is inevitable, so at least we can select a time and so outwit it.

The fact that all is conveyed on one level, in a monotone, does impose restraints, and force a justification of an eccentric technique. This technique has to lean on the author's power to accumulate and transmit detail, both in character and in situation, which are rendered vigorously. The effect of the monotone can be hypnotic as can the swing of the narrative in various directions and the shift different ways. But throughout all the crazy pastiche, flashes back and forward, tapestries of families and family circles, there does move a tragic sense, the memento mori most proudly borne by Goldmann, in the face of the self-indulgent, introspective lives of the strange but familiar figures that populate this novel.

BIBLIOGRAPHY

Chapter 1

Alter, R. *Defenses of the Imagination* (Philadelphia, 1977)
Ben-Horin, M. *Max Nordau: Philosopher of Human Solidarity* (London, 1956)
Berdyczewski, M.J. *Kol Kitvey* 2 vols. (Tel-Aviv, 1951)
Bialik, H.M. *Kol Kitvey* 4 vols. (Tel-Aviv, 1939)
Brenner, Y.H. *Kol Kitvey* 3 vols. (Tel-Aviv, 1957)
Brenner, Y.H. *Breakdown and Bereavement* (Ithaca, 1971)
Jabotinsky, Z. *Kol Kitvey* 16 vols. (Tel-Aviv, 1940)
Laqueur, W. *A History of Zionism* (London, 1972)
Mendeli Mocher Sefarim *Kol Kitvey* (Tel-Aviv, 1947)
Nordau, M. *Die convenzionellen Luegen Der Kulturmenscheit* 1883, *The Conventional Lies of our Civilisation*, 1884)
—— *Die Krankheit des Jahrhunderts* (1889)
—— *Entartung* (1893, *Degeneration*, 1895)
—— Address to 1st Zionist Congress (republished Jerusalem, 1947)
Rejzen, Z. *Lexicon für der Yiddisher litèratur* (Vilna, 1926)
Schechtman, J. *Rebel and Statesman* (New York, 1956)
—— *Fighter and Prophet* (New York, 1961)
Schnitzler, A. *Jugend in Wien* (1968, *My Youth in Vienna* (1971) A diary from 1862 to 1889
—— *Reigen* (1900, *Merry-go-round*, 1952)
—— *Vienna 1900: Games with Love and Death* (London, 1973)
Schorske, C.E. *Fin-de-siècle Vienna: Politics and Culture* (London, 1961)

Chapter 2

Cahan, A. *The Rise of David Levinsky* (New York, 1917, 1960)
Fiedler, L. *The Jew in the American Novel* (New York, 1959)
Fuchs, D. *Summer in Williamsburg* (New York, 1934, 1961)
—— *Homage to Blenholt* (New York, 1936, 1961)
Gartner, L.P. 'Immigration and the Formation of American Jewry, 1840-1925' in H. Ben-Sasson and S. Ettinger (eds.), *Jewish Society through the Ages* (London, 1971)

Gold, M. *120 Million* (New York, 1929)
—— *Jews without Money* (New York, 1930)
Guttmann, A. *The Jewish Writer in America* (New York, 1971)
Hecht, B. *A Jew in Love* (New York, 1931)
Howe, I. *The Immigrant Jews of New York* (London, 1976); published
    as *The World of our Fathers* in New York
Levin, M. *In Search* (New York, 1950)
Lewisohn, L. *The Island Within* (New York, 1928)
Roth, H. *Call it Sleep* (New York, 1934; London, 1963, 1976)
Scott, H.G. (ed.) *Problems of Soviet Literature* (London, 1935)

Chapter 3

Brod, M. *Franz Kafka: A Biography* (Prague, 1937, New York, 1960)
Buber, M. *Ich und Du* (Berlin, 1922) *I and Thou* (London, 1937)
Davidowicz, L. *The War against the Jews 1933-45* (New York, 1975)
Diamond, M.L. *Martin Buber, Jewish Existentialist* (New York, 1960)
Gay, P. *Weimar Culture: The Outsider as Insider* (New York, 1968)
Glatzer, N.N. (presented by) *Franz Rosenzweig* (New York, 1953,
    1961)
Heller, E. *Kafka* (London, 1974)
Kafka, F. *Das Schloss* (Munich, 1921) *The Castle* (London, 1930)
—— *Der Prozess* (Berlin, 1925) *The Trial* (London, 1933)
—— *Amerika* (Munich, 1927) *America* (London, 1938)
—— *Parables and Paradoxes* (Berlin, 1935; New York, 1961)
—— *Diaries* (London, 1948)
—— *Wedding Preparations in the Country and other Stories* (London,
    1954)
Laqueur, E. *The Weimar Republic: A Cultural History 1918-1933*
    (London, 1974)
McKenzie, J.R.P. *Weimar Germany 1918-1933* (New Jersey, 1971)
Rosenzweig, F. *Der Stern der Erlösung* (Frankfurt, 1921) *The Star of
    Redemption* (London, 1971)
Scholem, G. *From Berlin to Jerusalem* (Berlin, 1977; New York, 1979)

Chapter 4

Babel, I. *Collected Stories* (London, 1957)
—— *Lyubka the Cossack and Other Stories* (New York, 1963)

—— *Benya Krik the Gangster and Other Stories* (London, 1971)
Ehrenburg, I. *Russia at War* (London, 1943)
Friedberg, M. 'Jewish Contrbution to Soviet Literature' in L. Kochan
(ed.), *The Jews in Soviet Russia since 1917* (London 1970a)
—— 'Jewish Themes in Soviet Literature' in L. Kochan (ed.), *The Jews in Soviet Russia since 1917* (London, 1970b)
Gilbert, M. *The Jews of Russia: Their History in Maps* (London, 1976)
Ginzburg, E. *Into the Whirlwind* (London, 1967)
Hingley, R. *Russian Writers and Soviet Society* (London, 1979)
Ilf, I. and Petrov, Y. *The Twelve Chairs* (New York, 1961)
Labedz, L. and Hayward, M. *On Trial: The Case of Sinyavsky (Tertz) and Daniel (Arghak)* (London, 1967)
Mandelstam, N. *Hope against Hope* (London, 1970)
—— *Hope Abandoned* (London, 1973)
Mandelstam, O. *The Prose of Osip Mandelstam* (Princeton, 1965)
—— *Selected Poems* (London, 1973)
Pasternak, B. *Doctor Zhivago* (London, 1958)
Sachar, H. *The Course of Modern Jewish History* (New York, 1955)
Tertz, A. *The Trial Begins* (London, 1960)

Chapter 5

Agnon, S.Y. *Kol Sipurov,* 7 vols. (Jerusalem and Tel-Aviv, 1960)
—— *Shirah* (Jerusalem and Tel-Aviv, 1971)
Bein, A. *The Return to the Soil* (Jerusalem, 1952)
Bialik, H.N. *Kitvey,* 4 vols. (Tel-Aviv, 1965)
Burla, Y. *Kitvey,* 8 vols. (Tel-Aviv, undated)
—— *In Darkness Striving* (Tel-Aviv, 1968)
Gilbert M. *The Jews of Russia* (London, 1976)
Greenberg, U.Z. *Eymah Gedolah Weyareah* (Tel-Aviv, 1924)
—— *Hagavrut Haolah* (Tel-Aviv, 1926)
—— *Anaqreon al Qotev Haitzavon* (Tel-Aviv, 1928)
—— *Rehovoth Hanahar* (Tel-Aviv, 1951)
Hazaz, H. *Kol Kitvey,* 12 vols. (Tel-Aviv, 1970)
—— *Mishpat Hageulah* (Tel-Aviv, 1977)
Hochman, B. *The Fiction of S.Y. Agnon* (Ithaca, 1970)
Laqueur, W. *A History of Zionism* (London, 1972)
Patai, R. *Israel between East and West* (Philadelphia, 1955)
Yudkin, L.I. *Escape into Siege* (London, 1974)

Chapter 6

Bensimon, D. 'Socio-demographic aspects of French Jewry', *European Judaism,* 1978, no. 1

Bessy, M. *Car c'est Dieu qu'on Enterre* (Paris, 1960)

Blot, J. 'The Jewish novel in France', *European Judaism,* 1970, no. 1

Cohen, A. *Le Livre de ma Mère* (Paris, 1954)

de Boisdeffre, P. 'Y-a-t-il un roman juif?', *L'Arche*, December 1979

Fleg, E. *Pourquoi je suis Juif* (Paris, 1927, 1945)

—— *Écoute, Israël: Et tu aimeras L'Eternel* (Paris, 1935, 1948)

Guide Juif de France (Paris, 1971)

Mandel, A. *Tikoun* (Paris, 1980)

Memmi, A. *Le Statue de Sel* (Paris, 1953)

—— *Portrait d'un Juif* (Paris, 1962, 1966)

—— *Juifs et Arabes* (Paris, 1974)

Neher, A. 'L'esprit de Judaisme française', *L'Arche*, August-September 1960

Rais, E. 'Poètes Juifs d'expression Francaise', *Le Monde Juif,* August-September 1949

—— 'Les écrivains juifs d'expression Française', *Le Monde Juif,* February 1950

Schwarz-Bart, A. *Le Dernier des Justes* (Paris, 1959), *The Last of the Just,* London, 1961)

Sperber, M. *Plus Profond que L'abîme* (Paris, 1950)

Spire, A. *Poèmes Juifs* (Paris, 1959)

Chapter 7

Bashevis-Singer, I. *The Manor* (New York, 1967)

—— *The Estate* (New York, 1969)

Bellow, S. *Dangling Man* (New York, 1944)

—— *Herzog* (New York, 1964)

—— *Mr Sammler's Planet* (New York, 1970)

Grade, C. *The Agunah* (New York, 1974)

Mailer, N. *The Naked and the Dead* (New York, 1948)

—— *Barbary Shore* (New York, 1951)

—— *Advertisements for Myself* (New York, 1960)

—— *An American Dream* (New York, 1965)

—— *The Armies of the Night* (New York, 1968)

Malamud, B. *The Assistant* (New York, 1957)

—— *The Magic Barrel* (New York, 1958)
—— *The Fixer* (New York, 1960)
—— *Dubin's Lives* (New York, 1979)
Potok, C. *The Chosen* (New York, 1967)
—— *The Promise* (New York, 1969)
Roth, P. *Goodbye Columbus* (New York, 1959)
—— *Portnoy's Complaint* (New York, 1969)
Styron, W. *Sophie's Choice* (New York, 1979)
Trilling, L. *The Middle of the Journey* (New York, 1947)

Chapter 8

Bassani, G. *Il giardino dei Finzi-Contini* (1962, *The Garden of the Finzi-Continis*, translated by Isabel Quigley, 1965)
—— *Dietro la porta* (1964, *Behind the Door*, translated by William Weaver, 1972)
Caredio, A. M. *Amo Israele* (Siena, 1969)
Centro di Documentalia Ebraica Contemporanea, *Gli Ebrei in Italia*, no. 2 (Milan, 1962)
Della-Pergura, S. *Anatomia dell ebraismo italiano* (Rome, 1976)
Ginzburg, N. *Mai devi domandarmi* (Rome, 1970, *Never Must You Ask Me*, translated by Isabel Quigley, 1973)
Levi, P. *Se questo e un Uomo* (Rome, 1947, *If this is a Man*, translated by Stuart Woolf, 1960)
—— *La tregua* (Rome, 1963, *The Truce*, translated by Stuart Woolf, 1965)
—— *Shema: collected poems* (translated by Ruth Feldman, London, 1976)
Michaellis, M. *Mussolini and the Jews* (Oxford, 1978)
Milano, A. *Storia degli ebrei in Italia* (Turin, 1963)
Millu, L. *Il fumo di Birkenau* (Florence, 1947)
Moravia, A. *Gli indifferenti* (Rome, 1929, *The Time of Indifference*, London, 1953)
—— *La mascherata* (Rome, 1940, *The Fancy-dress Party*, London, 1947)
—— *L'amore coniugale* (Rome, 1949, *Conjugal Love*, London, 1951)
—— *Il conformista* (Rome, 1951, *The Conformist*, London 1952)
—— *Il depresso* (Rome, 1955, *A Ghost at Noon*, London, 1955)
—— *La ciociara* (Rome, 1957, *Two Women*, London, 1958)

Reitlinger, G. *The Final Solution* (London, 1953)

Romano, G. 'The Jewish Novel in Italy', *European Judaism*, 1970, vol. 1

Roth, C. *The History of the Jews in Italy* (London, 1946)

Schirman, H. *Mivhar Lashirah Laivrit beitalyah* (Berlin, 1934)

Chapter 9

Amichai, Y. *Baruah Hanoraah Hazoth* (Tel-Aviv, 1961)

—— *Shirim* (Tel-Aviv, 1967)

—— *Selected Poems* (London, 1971)

—— *Travels of a Latter-Day Benjamin of Tudela* (London, 1977)

—— *Amen,* (Oxford, 1978)

Appelfeld, A. *Shanim Weshaoth* (Tel-Aviv, 1975)

Encyclopaedia Judaica (Jerusalem, 1971 vol. 9, article 'Israel, State of'

Oz, A. *My Michael* (London, 1972)

—— *Elsewhere Perhaps* (New York, 1973)

—— *Touch the Water, Touch the Wind* (New York, 1974)

—— *The Hill of Evil Counsel* (London, 1978)

Shabtai, Y. *Zikhron Dvarim* (Tel-Aviv, 1977)

Shamir, M. *Hu Halakh Basadoth* (Tel-Aviv, 1947)

—— *Thahath Hashamesh* (Tel-Aviv, 1950)

—— *Bemo Yadaw* (Tel-Aviv, 1951)

—— *Hagvul* (Tel-Aviv, 1950)

Yizhar, S. *Arbaah Sipurim* (Tel-Aviv, 1950)

—— *Midnight Convoy* (Tel-Aviv, 1969)

*All Moravia works cited here are translated by Angus Davidson.

INDEX

aesthetics 12
Agnon, S.Y. 81-4
Alter, R. 12
Alterman, N. 85, 156
Amichai, Y. 145, 148-52
Amir, A. 144
Ansky, S. 17
anti-semitism 11, 22, 45
Appelfeld, A. 156
Austria 45

Babel, I. 61, 62, 68-71
Bashevis-Singer, I. 126
Bassani, G. 135-7
Bein, A. 85
Bellow, S. 113, 115-18, 123
Ben-Amotz, D. 156
Ben-Horin, M. 21
Benjamin, W. 151
Berdyczewski, M.J. 15-17
Bessy, M. 110
Bialik, H.N. 13, 78-81
Brenner, Y.H. 24-6
Brod, M. 49
Buber, M. 55, 57-8
Bundism 13, 59
Burla, Y. 91-4

Cahan, A. 28-32
Canaanism 143
Caredio, A.M. 140
Cohen, A. 98, 109-10
Czechoslovakia 45

Daniel, Y. 72
Davidowicz, L. 45
Dor, M. 143, 145

Ehrenburg, I. 61, 74-5, 77
English 10
Enlightenment 11
Expressionism 46

Fiedler, L. 28
Fleg, E. 100, 100-2, 111
Forward 29

France 10, 11
Friedberg, M. 60
Fuchs, D. 29, 40-1

Gartner, L.P. 27
Gay, P. 46
German 10, 11
Gilbert, M. 60, 78
Ginzburg, E. 64, 76
Ginzburg, N. 131-3
Gogol, N. 61
Gold, M. 35-7
Grade, C. 126
Greenberg, U.Z. 85-8, 156
Guttmann, A. 28

Hasidism 13
Hazaz, H. 88-91, 144
Hebrew 11, 13
Hecht, B. 29, 37
Heller, E. 48
Herzl, T. 23, 97
Howe, I. 30
Hrushowski, B. 145

Ilf, I. 76-7
Israel 10
Italy 10

Jabotinsky, V. 10, 17-19

Kafka, F. 47-53, 81
Kahana-Carmon, A. 156
Karni, Y. 85
Kenan, A. 144
Kenaz, Y. 156
Kurzweil, B. 148

Lamdan, Y. 85, 147
Laqueur, W. 45, 47
Levi, P. 138-40
Lewisohn, L. 10, 29, 32-5
Lilienblum, M. 127
Luxemburg, R. 46

Mailer, N. 118-21

Malamud, B. 113, 121-3
Mandel, A. 111
Mandelstam, N. 62-4
Mandelstam, O. 62, 65-8
Megged, A. 156
Memmi, A. 105-7, 111
Mendeli 13-15
Millu, L. 141
Moravia, A. 133-5

Neher, A. 98
Nordau, M. 20-1, 97

Oz, A. 153-6

Palestine 10
Pasternak, B. 62, 63, 71-4
Poland 59
Potok, C. 126-8

Quigly, I. 131

Rais, E. 99
Rathenau, W. 46
Ratosh, Y. 144
Reform 13
Reitlinger, G. 130
Rejzen, Z. 13
Romano, G. 141
Rosenzweig, F. 54-7
Roth, C. 129, 130
Roth, H. 28, 41-4

Roth, P. 113, 123-6
Russia 10

Sachar, H. 58
Schirman, H. 141
Schnitzler, A. 22-4
Schwarz-Bart, A. 107-9
Shabtai, Y. 156-8
Shamir, M. 143, 145-6, 147, 156
Shlonsky, A. 85
Sinyavsky, A. 77
Sivan, A. 143, 145
Socialism 13
Sperber, M. 111
Spire, A. 100, 102-5, 111
Stalin, J. 62
Styron, W. 113

Tammuz, B. 144
Tolstoy, L. 61
Trilling, L. 113-15, 119

Wiesel, E. 99

Yiddish 10, 11, 13, 126
Yizhar, S. 144, 147-8
Yudkin, L.I. 79

Zach, N. 143, 145
Zhdanov, A. 35
Zionism 13, 59